CHAEREAS
AND CALLIRHOE

. . . is the earliest Greek romantic
novel the text of which has been
completely preserved; hence it is
among the first ancestors of modern
European fiction. A lively tale of
adventure, in which a nobly born
heroine is kidnapped across the seas
from Syracuse to Asia Minor, where
her beauty causes many complica-
tions and she is finally rescued by her
dashing lover, this book in antiquity
took the place of such stories as
Dumas and Sabatini have written
for later generations.

CHARITON'S

CHAEREAS and CALLIRHOE

CHARITON'S

CHAEREAS AND CALLIRHOE

TRANSLATED FROM THE GREEK BY

WARREN E. BLAKE

ASSOCIATE PROFESSOR OF GREEK

UNIVERSITY OF MICHIGAN

ANN ARBOR: UNIVERSITY OF MICHIGAN PRESS

LONDON: HUMPHREY MILFORD, OXFORD UNIVERSITY PRESS

MCMXXXIX

PRINTED IN THE

UNITED STATES OF AMERICA

BY EVANS-WINTER-HEBB INC., DETROIT, MICHIGAN

PREFACE

THIS *novel, while not the first one ever written, is nevertheless the first in European history to survive intact to our day. Consequently, its author, Chariton of Aphrodisia, can take his modest place among the many Greeks who individually are the originators or prototypes of one or more phases of our intellectual background.*

Our information about Chariton is extremely scanty. In the opening sentence of his novel he gives us his name and tells us that his home-town was Aphrodisia, a city of Caria in southern Asia Minor, and that he was secretary to a professional pleader in the courts, named Athenagoras. The discovery of inscriptions at the modern site of Aphrodisia bearing the names "Chariton" and "Athenagoras" confirms at least the existence of such families in that district, and as for his occupation, we need only to think of Charles Lamb among others of modern times to recognize in Chariton the type of conscientious clerical worker whose leisure was devoted to writing.

In view of the complete absence in ancient literature of any certain allusion to Chariton, he was long supposed to be the latest of the authors of Greek romance, and was dated, purely by conjecture, about 500 A.D. But by a turn of fortune as truly remarkable as any attributed by Chariton himself to that fickle goddess, three scraps of his book have been turned up in Egypt during the last forty years. One of these scraps was found in company with some business documents which date from about the end of the second century of our era. Inasmuch as the place of discovery was a small country town to which new works of literature would not likely penetrate immediately on publication, and since in any case an expensive book is almost sure to be preserved longer than day-by-day business papers, we seem quite justified in setting the date of publication back some twenty-five or even fifty years. Thus it is probable that this novel was written at least as early as the middle of the second century, only about one hundred years later than most of the books of the New Testament.

Chariton therefore is now restored to his rightful place as the earliest

v

*surviving representative of the romance-writers of Greece, and by conse-
quence, of the Western world. As such his importance in the history of
the novel can hardly be exaggerated.*

*The present English translation is the first to be made directly from
the Greek text. Its only predecessor, of anonymous authorship and dating
from 1764, was based upon an Italian translation of the imperfect text
of the first Greek edition. In preparing his version the translator has used
the most recent text edition, edited by himself and published at Oxford
in 1938. Reference numbers to the sections of the Greek text have here
been omitted in the belief that the advantage to the general reader of a
smoothly continuous page more than offsets the possible inconvenience
to the few who may wish to compare specific passages of the translation
with the original. For the latter the full analytical index of the text edition
will suffice. For like reasons identification by book and verse of the twenty-
seven quotations from Homer (here based on the translation of Lang,
Leaf, and Myers for the* Iliad, *and on that of Butcher and Lang for the*
Odyssey) *and by fragment numbers of the four quotations from Men-
ander and other comic poets, has also been left in the index to the Greek
text. The translator has tried to combine faithful reproduction of every
turn of thought in the original with a somewhat brittle, modern idiom,
designed to recapture as far as possible Chariton's abrupt and rapid-
moving style. His hope has been to reintroduce to modern readers a really
good story which at the same time happens to be the earliest representative of all the good stories which, in the form of novels, have amused the
world for the last eighteen hundred years.*

*To the numerous friends and colleagues who have read the manu-
script in whole or in part and have made suggestions for improvement the
translator is most grateful, and especially to Dr. Frank E. Robbins, who
with a delicate sense of style has helped to remove many an infelicity from
the text, and with great patience and skill has dealt with the many prob-
lems involved in putting the work through the press.*

*Grateful acknowledgment is made also to Mr. Dexter M. Ferry, Jr.,
of Detroit, the donor of the fund which makes this publication possible.*

W. E. B.

CONTENTS

•

BOOK I

BOOK I

I AM Chariton of Aphrodisia, secretary to the advocate Athenagoras, and I am going to tell you about a love affair that took place in Syracuse. Hermocrates, general of Syracuse, the one who defeated the Athenians, had a daughter named Callirhoe, a wonderful sort of girl and the admiration of all Sicily. Really her loveliness was hardly human; it was divine,—and it was not that of a mere nymph of the sea or the mountains, either, but of Aphrodite the Maiden. The fame of this incredible vision of beauty spread far and wide and suitors came pouring into Syracuse, potentates and royal princes, not only from Sicily, but from Italy, Epirus, and the nations of the Asiatic continent. But the god of love wanted to make a match of his own devising.

Now there was a certain young man called Chaereas, better looking than all the rest, who resembled the statues and pictures of Achilles and Nireus and Hippolytus and Alcibiades. His father was Ariston, second in rank only to Hermocrates in Syracuse. There was a political rivalry between the two, which would have led either of them to make an alliance with any family sooner than with that of the other. However, Love thrives on opposition and delights in accomplishing unexpected results, and this was the opportunity for which he was looking.

There was a public festival of Aphrodite and almost all the women had gone off to her temple. Callirhoe until now had never appeared in public, but at her father's command, her mother brought her out to worship the goddess. Just then Chaereas was walking home from the gymnasium, radiant as a star. The flush of exercise bloomed on his glowing face like gold on silver. Now as it happened, these two came upon each other at a narrow corner face to face,—a meeting shrewdly contrived by the god to insure their seeing each other. Immediately they fell in love, since beauty had met with nobility.

Like a hero mortally wounded in battle, ashamed to fall, but unable to stand, Chaereas could barely go off home with his wound. As for the girl, she fell at the feet of Aphrodite, kissed them, and said, "Lady, give me as my husband this man whom thou hast shown me!"

Night came on, dreadful to both, for love's fire was kindled. Yet the girl's suffering was more severe because she had to keep silent in shame of being

3

discovered. But when Chaereas began to waste away, being a young man of good disposition and proud spirit, he had the courage to tell his parents that he was in love and could not live unless he won Callirhoe as his wife. On hearing this, his father groaned and said, "My boy, your case is hopeless. Hermocrates, I am sure, would never give you his daughter when she has so many other suitors of wealth and royal rank. No, you must not even attempt it, or we may be openly insulted."

His father then tried to comfort the boy, but his trouble grew, so that he no longer appeared in public to engage in his usual pursuits. The gymnasium felt the loss of Chaereas and was practically deserted, for the young people loved him. By persistent inquiry they learned the cause of his illness, and they all felt sincere pity for this handsome young man who was in danger of death from the honest passion of his heart.

A formal public assembly was called. When the people had taken their seats, their first and only demand was this, "Noble Hermocrates, mighty general, save Chaereas! Let this be the greatest of your triumphs. Our city intercedes for the marriage today of these two who are so worthy of each other."

Who could describe that assembly of which the god of love was the spokesman? Hermocrates, as a true patriot, was unable to refuse the demands of the state. So when he nodded his assent, all the people leaped to their feet and ran from the theater. The young men went off after Chaereas while the senators and officials followed along with Hermocrates. Even the women of Syracuse were there to conduct the bride to her home. The marriage hymn was chanted throughout all the city, the narrow lanes were filled with garlands and torches, and the vestibules were sprinkled with wine and perfumes. The Syracusans celebrated this day with greater delight than the day of their victory.

Now the girl knew nothing of this and had thrown herself with covered head upon her couch, silently weeping. Her nurse came to her bed and said, "Get up, my child. The day has come which we all have wanted most. The city is celebrating your wedding."

"Her knees and heart were unstrung," as Homer says, for she did not know to whom she was being married. Immediately she became speechless, and a blackness spread over her eyes and she nearly fainted. To those that saw her, this appeared to be her modesty. But as soon as her maids had dressed her, the crowd at her doors went away, and the parents of the bridegroom brought him to the girl. And so Chaereas ran forward and kissed her, and Callirhoe, recognizing her lover, became more stately and lovely than ever, as a flickering lamp again flares up when oil is poured in.

When she went out to appear in public, astonishment overcame all the crowd just as when Artemis appears to hunters in lonely places. Indeed, many of those present even fell down to worship her. All admired Callirhoe and congratulated

Chaereas. The wedding was much like that of Thetis, which, as the poets sing, took place in Pelion. Yet here, too, was found a demon of envy just as there, they say, was the goddess of strife.

The suitors who had failed to win the bride felt both grief and anger. Though hitherto they had quarreled with each other, they now came to an understanding, and through this understanding and a sense of the insult they had received, they joined in common counsel, and envy was their leader in their attack upon Chaereas.

First a young man from Italy, the prince of Rhegium, stood up and spoke as follows: "If any one of us had married her, I should not have been angry, for, just as in the athletic games, one man only among the contestants must be the victor; but since he has surpassed us without working to win his bride, I cannot bear the insult. As for us, we have wasted away, keeping sleepless nights before the door of her house, flattering nurses and maids, and sending gifts to her attendants. How long we have been slaves! And what is worst of all, we have come to hate each other as rivals. But this dirty rascal, poverty-stricken and the lowest of the low, in a contest with kings has borne off the crown for himself without a struggle. Let us see to it that he does not enjoy his prize, and let us turn the wedding into death for the groom."

They all applauded, and only the ruler of Agrigentum objected. "It is not," he said, "through any good will toward Chaereas that I am holding up your plans against him, but through considerations of greater safety. Remember that Hermocrates is not a man lightly to be despised, so that it is impossible for us to attack him openly. A crafty approach is better, for it is by unscrupulous deceit rather than brute force that we obtain power. Elect me general of this campaign against Chaereas and I promise you I will dissolve the marriage. I shall arm Jealousy against him, and she, with Love as her ally, can accomplish serious damage. Callirhoe may be even-tempered and incapable of low-minded suspicions, but Chaereas, trained as he is in the gymnasia and not inexperienced in youthful follies, can easily be made suspicious and thus fall into youthful jealousy. Also it is easier to approach him and speak with him."

While he was still talking, they all voted approval of his plan and intrusted the execution of it to him as a man of infinite resource. This then was the scheme on which he set to work.

It was evening, and a messenger came reporting that Ariston, Chaereas' father, had fallen from a ladder on his farm and that there was very little hope of his surviving. Though Chaereas was very fond of his father, he was even more distressed when he heard this, because he had to go alone, since it was not as yet proper to take his bride out with him.

During that night, while no one dared to visit his house in open revelry, yet men did come secretly and unobserved and quietly left behind them the evidence of a wild celebration. They hung wreaths upon the vestibule and sprinkled it with perfumes; they soaked the ground with wine and tossed half-burned torches about.

Day dawned and every passer-by stopped with the universal instinct of curiosity. Now that his father was feeling more comfortable, Chaereas was hurrying back to his wife. Seeing the crowd before the door, he was at first astonished, but when he learned the cause, he rushed in as though possessed. Finding the chamber still shut, he knocked vigorously. But when the maid had opened the door and he had stumbled in to Callirhoe's presence, his anger was changed to sorrow and he tore his clothes and shed tears. When she asked him what had happened, he was speechless, being able neither to disbelieve what he had seen, nor yet to believe what was so contrary to his wishes.

As he stood confused and trembling, his wife, quite unsuspicious of what had happened, begged him to tell her the reason for his anger. With bloodshot eyes and thick voice he said, "It is the fact that you have so quickly forgotten me that hurts so much," and he reproached her for the celebration.

But she, being the daughter of a general and full of pride, grew angry at the unjustice of the accusation and said, "There has been no celebration to disgrace my father's house. Perhaps your vestibule may be used to such things, and your dear friends may be resenting your marriage."

Saying this she turned away and covered her head, and the tears welled forth. Yet reconciliation between lovers is easy and they gladly accept any apology from each other. Thus Chaereas, changing his tone, began to coax and flatter her, and his wife quickly accepted his repentance with joy. This increased the ardor of their love all the more, and the parents of both congratulated themselves when they saw the oneness of mind of their children.

When his first device had fallen through, the suitor from Agrigentum then engaged upon another more effective one, and this was the nature of his contrivance. He had a dependent who was ready of speech and full of every social grace. He gave orders to him to act the part of a lover, since he was trying to make a friendly accomplice of Callirhoe's favorite maid whom she most highly valued of all her servants. After some difficulty this person succeeded in winning the girl over with generous gifts, and by declaring that unless he gained her love he would hang himself. A woman is easily taken in when she thinks that she is loved.

After making these preparations, the director of this drama discovered another actor, not equally attractive, but a clever rascal and a persuasive talker. When he had given him preliminary instructions as to what he must do and say, he sent him secretly to Chaereas as a stranger.

Coming up to him as he was wandering about near the wrestling grounds, he said, "Chaereas, I too had a son of just your age who greatly admired and loved you when he was alive. Now that he is dead, I consider you as my son,—indeed, you and your happiness are a common blessing to all Sicily. Give me a little of your time and you shall hear of important matters which concern your whole life."

With these words this abominable rogue set the young man's heart aflutter and filled him with hope, fear, and curiosity. But when he begged him to speak, the other hesitated and pretended that the present occasion was not suitable and that they needed further delay and a longer time. Chaereas insisted all the more, expecting by now something rather serious.

The other took him by the right hand and led him off to a quiet spot. Then, contracting his brows, and assuming an expression of sorrow, and shedding a few tears besides, he said, "Chaereas, it is not pleasant for me to tell you of this sad business, and though I long have wanted to speak, I have hesitated. But now that you are being openly disgraced and the horrible thing is being discussed everywhere, I can no longer stand it to keep quiet. I am a man who naturally hates wrong, and I feel especially kindly toward you. You must know then that your wife is a partner in adultery and, to prove this to you, I am ready to show you the adulterer in the very act."

"Thus spake he, and a black cloud of grief enwrapped him, and with both hands he took dark dust and poured it over his head and defiled his comely face." For a long time Chaereas remained in a daze, unable to speak or raise his eyes. When he had recovered, he said in a voice that was unnatural and weak, "It is a miserable favor indeed to ask of you, to make me an eye-witness of my own troubles. Yet show him to me so that I may have greater reason for killing myself, for even though Callirhoe is guilty too, I shall spare her."

"Pretend," said the other, "that you are going away to the country. Then late in the evening keep watch on the house and you shall see her lover go in."

So they agreed, and Chaereas sent in a messenger, since he could not endure even to go in there himself, and said, "I am going away to the country." Then the black-hearted villain set the scene of his drama.

When evening came, Chaereas took his place of observation while the other man, who had corrupted Callirhoe's maid, darted up the narrow lane, acting as though he preferred to get at his business in secret, but actually managing it all so as not to be overlooked. He had long lustrous hair with locks scented with perfume; his eyes were lined with cosmetics; his cloak was soft; his shoes were light and fine; heavy rings gleamed on his fingers. Next, looking carefully around, he approached the door and knocking lightly, gave the usual sign. The maid, also in great trepidation, softly opened the door and taking him by the hand, led him in. Seeing this, Chaereas could no longer restrain himself but rushed in to seize the

7

adulterer on the spot. He, however, had taken his stand beside the door of the courtyard and quickly ran out.

Callirhoe was sitting on her couch longing for Chaereas and had not even lighted a lamp because of her sorrow. There came the sound of footsteps and she was first aware of her husband by his heavy breathing, and ran with joy to greet him. But he had no voice with which to reproach her; instead, overwhelmed with anger, he kicked at his wife as she ran forward, and his foot struck her squarely in the middle and stopped short her breath. She fell on the floor and her maidservants picked her up and laid her upon the bed. And so Callirhoe lay without speech or breath, presenting to all the appearance of death.

Rumor ran throughout the city reporting what had happened, and aroused cries of grief throughout the narrow streets down to the sea. From every side lamentations resounded, and the affair was very like the capture of a city. Chaereas, still inwardly seething, locked himself in a room and throughout the night severely examined the maidservants, first and last Callirhoe's favorite, and he learned the truth in the course of torturing them with fire and whips. Then his heart was overcome with pity for his dead wife and he longed to kill himself, but was prevented by Polycharmus, a particular friend of his, just as Patroclus was to Achilles in Homer.

When day came, the officials empaneled a jury for the murder trial, hurrying the case out of respect for Hermocrates. The whole populace, too, rapidly assembled in the market place, with various shouts and exclamations. The unsuccessful suitors sought the favor of the crowd, and especially the man from Agrigentum, with the imposing and dignified manner of one who has accomplished some utterly unexpected result.

A strange thing now took place, the like of which had never before occurred in a courtroom. After the charge had been made, the murderer, instead of defending himself when his time had been allotted him by the water clock, brought still more bitter accusations against himself and was the first to cast the vote of condemnation. He said nothing that was appropriate to his defense, not mentioning the slanderous attack, nor his jealousy, nor his lack of premeditation, but begged them all, "Stone me to death in public. I have robbed our people of their crown. It is an act of mercy if you hand me over to the executioner. This ought to be my fate if it were only a maidservant of Hermocrates whom I had killed. Look for some unspeakable kind of punishment. I have committed a crime worse than temple-robbing or parricide. Do not bury me. Do not pollute the earth but sink my sinful body in the depths of the sea!"

At these words a cry of grief broke forth and every one deserted the cause of the dead woman and mourned for the living man.

Hermocrates was the first to counsel Chaereas. "I know," he said, "that what happened was unintended. I have my eyes on the conspirators. They shall not enjoy the sight of two corpses, and I shall not offend the memory of my daughter. Indeed I have heard her say many times that she had rather Chaereas should live than herself. Let us put a stop to this useless court trial and go out to the tomb that none may escape. Let us not give up her body to the ravages of time nor allow it to lose its beauty through decay. Let us bury Callirhoe while she is still beautiful."

Accordingly the jury cast the vote of acquittal. Chaereas, however, would not acquit himself but longed for death and was arranging every means of accomplishing his end. Polycharmus, seeing that it was impossible to save him in any other way, said, "Traitor to the dead, will you not wait even to bury Callirhoe? Will you trust her body to the hands of others? Now is the time for you to provide rich funeral offerings and to prepare a royal funeral procession." This speech was persuasive, for it inspired in him feelings of pride and responsibility.

Who could worthily describe that funeral procession? Callirhoe, clothed in her bridal garments, lay upon a golden bier, more stately and beautiful than ever, so that they all compared her to the sleeping Ariadne. Ahead of the bier came first the knights of Syracuse, themselves and their horses in full regalia; after them were heavy-armed soldiers carrying the standards of Hermocrates' triumphs; then the senate; and in the center, the assembly, all acting as bodyguards to Hermocrates. Ariston, too, was carried along, since he was still weak, and he called Callirhoe his daughter and mistress. After these were the women of the citizens clad in black; next, a royal wealth of funeral offerings, first the gold and silver of the dowry, a beautiful array of clothing (for Hermocrates had contributed much from the spoils of war), and the gifts of relatives and friends. Last of all followed the rich possessions of Chaereas, since it was his wish, if possible, to burn all his property at the burial of his wife. The young men of Syracuse carried the bier and the rabble followed behind. Amid the lamentations of all, the voice of Chaereas was distinctly heard.

There was a magnificent tomb belonging to Hermocrates near the shore, so as to be visible even to people far out at sea. This was filled like a treasure-house with the abundant richness of the funeral gifts. However, what was intended to serve as a mark of respect to the dead, brought about the beginning of still greater happenings.

There was a rascal called Theron who followed a criminal career upon the sea. He was in command of freebooters who secretly rode at anchor in the harbors, pretending to be ferry-men, and thus he organized his business of piracy. He had happened to be present at the funeral procession and had fixed his eyes on the gold, and at night when he lay down to sleep he could not rest.

"Am I to risk my life," he said to himself, "battling with the sea and committing murders for a mere pittance when there is a chance to get rich from one lone corpse? No! It is settled. I will not pass by this profit. But whom shall I enlist for this business? Think carefully, Theron. Who of those you know is fit for the job? Zenophanes, of Thurium? He is shrewd, but he is a coward. Menon of Messenia? He is daring enough, but a traitor." Going over each man in his thoughts, and as it were, testing their metal, he rejected most of them, but considered a few as suitable.

At early dawn he ran down to the harbor and looked up each of them. Some he found in the brothels and some in the taverns, a gang well worthy of such a leader. Saying that he had something of great importance to tell them, he led them off back of the harbor and began with these words: "I have found a treasure, and I have chosen you of all men to share it with me. There is no mere one-man profit in this, and yet there is not much effort required either, but a single night's work can make us all rich. We are no strangers to business of this sort, which fools may condemn, but sensible men may turn to advantage."

They understood at once that he was proposing some piece of piracy or tomb-breaking or temple-robbing and said, "Stop trying to persuade us when we are already persuaded. Just tell us what the business is, and let us not lose our time."

"You have seen the gold and silver with the corpse," said Theron in reply. "This should more rightly belong to us, the living. I propose to open up the tomb at night and then to load our boat and sail away wherever the wind may take us and sell our cargo in a foreign land."

They were delighted.

"Now," said he, "go back again to your usual occupations. Late in the evening each one of you come down to the boat bringing a builder's tool."

This they did, and Callirhoe and her fortunes met with a new and more dreadful sort of resurrection. When lack of food had produced in her some degree of recovery from her suspended animation, she slowly and gradually regained her breath. Then she began to stir, one limb after another, and opening her eyes she regained consciousness as though waking from sleep, and called Chaereas, thinking he was sleeping beside her. But when neither her husband nor her servants heard her, and everything remained deserted and dark, a shudder of horror came over the poor girl, unable as she was by any exercise of reason to guess the truth.

Scarcely had she awakened, when her hands touched the funeral wreaths and ribbons. Her movements created a rattling of gold and silver. There was a prevalent odor of spices. Then, at last, she recalled the blow she had received and the fall that resulted from it, and reluctantly and with anguish she recognized the tomb.

Thereupon she broke the silence with a shout, as loud as she could utter, crying, "I am alive! Save me!"

But when she had cried many times and nothing further occurred, she gave up all hope of rescue, and bending her head on her knees she lamented.

"Oh, dreadful fate!" she said. "I have been buried alive though I did no wrong, and I am to die a lingering death. They mourn me as dead, though I am well. Whom can I find to send them a message? Cruel Chaereas, I blame you, not for causing my death, but because you were so hasty in casting me out from the house. You should not have buried Callirhoe so soon, not even if she were really dead. But perhaps you already have plans for remarriage!"

While she was thus engaged in incoherent lamentation, Theron, waiting until midnight, was noiselessly approaching the tomb, stroking the water lightly with his oars. Stepping ashore first, he assigned the duties of his crew in this way. He dispatched four men to keep watch in case anyone should approach the place, to kill them if they could, otherwise to give notice of their arrival by signal. He and four others proceeded to the tomb. As for the rest (there were eleven altogether) he told them to wait on board the boat and to keep the oars poised so that if any emergency arose, they could quickly pick up those on shore and sail away.

When the crowbars were applied, and the pounding grew louder as they broke into the tomb, Callirhoe was seized all at once with fear, joy, grief, amazement, hope, and disbelief.

"What does this noise mean? Has some divinity come to seek me in my misery, as is common in the experience of the dying? Or is this not mere noise, but the voice of the gods below who are calling me to them? It is more likely that they are tomb-robbers. So this, too, has been added to my misfortunes! Wealth is useless to a corpse."

While she was still seeking some explanation, the robber bent his head and entered the tomb a little way. Callirhoe fell down before him in her desire to beg mercy, but he leaped back in terror and with a trembling voice shouted to his comrades, "Let us get out of here. Some ghost is on guard in there and will not let us come in."

Theron laughed him to scorn, calling him a coward and more of a corpse than the dead woman herself. Then he ordered another man to go in, and when no one dared to do so, he entered himself, holding out his sword before him.

At the gleam of the steel, Callirhoe shrank back into the extreme corner of the tomb in fear of death, and from there she begged him in a small voice, "Whoever you are, have mercy on me, for I have obtained no mercy from either husband or parents. Do not kill me now that you have rescued me."

Theron gained more courage and, being a shrewd man, realized the truth. He stood there in deep thought and at first planned to kill the girl, thinking she would prove a hindrance to the whole undertaking. But with an eye to possible profit, he quickly changed his mind and said to himself, "She too can be a part of the funeral treasure. There is plenty of silver and gold here, but the beauty of the girl is more valuable than all of this."

So taking her by the hand he led her out. Then calling his assistant he said, "Look, here is the ghost that scared you. A fine buccaneer you are, to be afraid of a woman. Keep watch of her now, for I intend to give her back to her parents. As for us, let us bring out the stuff that is stored inside, now that no longer even the corpse is guarding it."

When they had filled the boat with the loot, Theron ordered the guard to stand a little to one side with the girl. Then he put before them the question as to what to do with her.

Various and contradictory opinions were expressed and the first speaker said, "Comrades, we came for one thing and, as fortune would have it, it has turned out to be something better. Let us take advantage of it. We can get the business done without risk. I propose to leave the tomb treasure right here and to give Callirhoe back to her husband and father and say that we anchored near the place in the course of our regular fishing and that on hearing a cry we opened the tomb out of pity so as to rescue her from her imprisonment. Let us make the girl swear to give full support to our testimony. She will be glad to do so out of gratitude to the kind friends who saved her. Just think with what joy we shall fill all Sicily, and the big rewards we shall get! At the same time we shall be doing the honest thing in the sight of men and the pious thing in the sight of heaven."

But before he had finished, another objected. "Misguided fool," he said, "are you telling us to play the philosopher at this stage? Has robbing a tomb made decent people of us? Shall we show her mercy when her own husband refused to do so and killed her? She has done us no harm, you say. But she will do us the greatest possible harm. In the first place, if we give her back to her relatives, there is no telling what attitude they will take about the matter, and it is impossible for them not to suspect the reason for our coming to the tomb. Also, even if the girl's relatives do forego any punishment of us, still the public officials and the people themselves will not let off tomb-robbers who are convicted by the very wares they bring. The life we lead is not without danger in any case. Perhaps someone may say that it is more profitable to sell the girl, since she will fetch a high price because of her beauty. But this, too, has its dangers. Gold has no voice and silver will not tell where we got it. About them we can make up any story we want. But who can hide away property which has eyes, ears, and a tongue? And besides, hers is no mere human beauty to help us avoid detection. Shall we say that she is a slave? Who will believe that, once he sees her? Therefore, let us kill her right here and let us not carry around a living accusation against ourselves." Though many agreed with these words, Theron put neither proposition to the vote.

"Your proposal," he said, "is dangerous. You, on the other hand, are ruining our profit. I will sell the girl rather than kill her. While she is on sale she will keep quiet through fear, and once sold let her bring her charges, when we are no longer there. Get on board. Let us sail. It is already near dawn."

The ship, when it put to sea, rode splendidly, for they did not force their way against wind and waves, having no special course laid out before them. Every wind seemed favorable to them and stood at the stern.

Theron sought to comfort Callirhoe, trying to deceive her with all kinds of notions. But she was aware of her situation, and knew that she had been rescued in vain. She pretended, however, not to know this, but to believe him, in fear that after all he might kill her if she seemed resentful. So, saying that she could not endure the sea, she covered her head and wept.

"In this very sea, father," she said, "you once defeated three hundred warships of the Athenians, and now one small vessel is bearing off your daughter and you cannot help me. I am being carried away to a strange land and I, a girl of noble birth, must be a slave. Perhaps some Athenian master will buy the daughter of Hermocrates! How much better it would be for me to lie dead in the tomb! Then, at any rate, Chaereas would have been buried with me. But now we have been parted both in life and in death."

Such were her lamentations. Meantime the robbers sailed past the smaller islands and towns, since their cargo was not suited for poor men, but they were looking for persons of wealth. Presently they anchored down by a mole opposite the coast of Attica, where there was a spring of pure, abundant water and a pleasant meadow. Taking Callirhoe there from out the boat, they required her to refresh herself and to get a little rest from the sea, wishing to preserve her beauty.

When they were alone, they proceeded to consider what course they should now set, and one man said, "Athens is nearby, a great and prosperous city. There we shall find a great number of dealers and an abundance of wealthy men. You can see as many whole cities in Athens as there are men in a market place."

So they all thought it best to sail down to Athens.

But Theron did not care for the peculiar officiousness of that town. "Is it possible," he said, "that you have not heard of the meddlesome curiosity of the Athenians? They are a talkative people and fond of lawsuits, and in the harbor shysters without number will try to find out who we are and where we got this cargo. Vile suspicions will fill their evil minds. The Areopagus is near at hand and their officials are sterner than tyrants. We may well fear the Athenians more than the Syracusans. The proper place for us is Ionia, where, as you know, there is royal wealth which comes flowing in from mighty Asia, and the people there enjoy luxury and are easy-going. Also I expect to find some acquaintances of mine there."

So after drawing a supply of water and taking on provisions from some nearby freighters, they sailed straight for Miletus and on the third day they arrived at

13

an anchorage most suitable to receive them, about ten miles distant from the city.

Theron then gave orders to take out the oars from the boat and to construct a shelter for Callirhoe and to provide everything for her comfort. This he did not so much from compassion as from love of gain, and more as a trader than a pirate.

He himself hastened down to the town, taking with him two of his companions. Then, having no intention of seeking a purchaser openly nor of making his business the town talk, he tried to hurry through a private sale with no bargaining. But it proved hard to manage, inasmuch as the property was not suited for many people nor for the ordinary man at all, but rather for some wealthy and royal patron, and he was afraid to approach men of this sort.

Consequently, after considerable time had been wasted, he no longer dared to put up with the delay, but when night came, he was unable to sleep, and said to himself, "Theron, you are a fool. You have left behind your gold and silver for all these days in a deserted place as though you were the only pirate in existence. Don't you know that other pirates, also, sail the sea? Then, too, I am afraid that our own men may desert us and sail away. Remember, you did not enlist the most honest men in the world, who would keep faith with you, but rather the biggest rascals you knew. Well," he said, "go to sleep now if you must, but when day comes, hurry down to the boat and throw overboard that misplaced nuisance of a woman, and don't take on any more cargoes so hard to dispose of."

Falling asleep, he dreamed of seeing locked doors, and so he determined to hold on for that day. In the course of his wanderings, he took a seat in a certain workshop, his spirits in utter confusion. Meantime a crowd of men, both free and slave, was passing by, and in the midst of them a man of mature age, clothed in black and sad of face.

Theron rose to his feet (for man is by nature curious) and inquired of one of the attendants, "Who is this man?"

The other replied, "I think you must be a stranger or come from a long way off if you do not recognize Dionysius, a man who is far above all the rest of the Ionians in wealth, ancestry, and education, and a friend of the Great King besides."

"Then why is he wearing black?"

"His dearly beloved wife has died."

Theron sought to prolong the conversation further, now that he had found a man who was rich and romantically inclined, and so he refused to let him go, and inquired, "What position do you hold with him?"

"I am the manager of his whole estate," he replied, "and I am taking care of his daughter, too, a mere baby, left an untimely orphan by the death of her mother."

"And what is your name?"

"Leonas."

"How lucky that I met you, Leonas," he said. "I am a trader just now sailing in from Italy, and that is why I know nothing of affairs in Ionia. A lady of Sybaris, the wealthiest in the city, had a very beautiful maid whom she put up for sale, because she was jealous of her, and I bought her. You can profit by this, if you want to get yourself a nurse for the child (she is well enough trained for that), or if you should consider it worth while to win the good will of your master. You see, it is more to your advantage for him to have a slave he has bought than for him to bring in a stepmother for the girl over your head."

Leonas was delighted to hear this and said, "Heaven must have sent you to be my benefactor. You are displaying to me in daylight the very things I've dreamed of. Come to my house now and be my friend and guest. I can decide about taking this woman when I see whether she is a possession worthy of my master or is merely in our class."

When they came to the house, Theron was astonished at its size and magnificence, for it had been prepared to receive the Great King of Persia. Leonas told him to wait while he first attended to the needs of his master. Then he took him and brought him up to his own room, which was very much like that of a free man, and gave orders to set the table. Theron, a shrewd person and clever in adapting himself to every occasion, helped himself to the food and made himself agreeable to Leonas by frequently drinking to his health. This was partly to demonstrate his frank good nature, but still more to inspire confidence in their partnership. Meantime there was considerable conversation about the girl, and Theron kept praising her good character rather than her beauty, knowing that invisible qualities require an advocate, whereas appearance recommends itself.

"Let us go, then," said Leonas. "Show her to me."

"She is not here," he replied. "We avoided coming to the city because of the customs officials and our boat is anchored about ten miles away,"—and he described the place.

"You are anchored on our own estate," said Leonas, "and that is so much the better. Fortune is plainly bringing you to Dionysius. So let us go down to the farm, and you can recover from your voyage. Our country house nearby is luxuriously furnished."

Theron was still more delighted, thinking that the transaction would be easier in a lonely place than in the open market.

"Let us start out at dawn," he said, "you to the country house, and I to my ship, and I will bring the girl from there to you."

So they agreed and after shaking hands they parted. The night seemed long to both, since one was eager to buy and the other to sell.

On the following day Leonas sailed down the coast to the country house, at the same time bringing with him some money to establish his prior claim with the dealer. Theron meanwhile arrived at the beach and was warmly welcomed by his confederates. After telling them what he had done, he began to coax Callirhoe.

"My daughter," said he, "at first I wanted to take you back to your people but when a contrary wind came up, I was completely prevented by the condition of the sea. I want you to realize what great care I have taken of you. Most important of all, I have preserved your honor. Chaereas shall get you back unharmed and saved by us, as it were, from the chamber of the tomb. Now we must continue our course to Lycia, but there is no need for you to undergo pointless hardships, especially when you suffer so from seasickness. And so I am going to entrust you to faithful friends here and when I come back I will pick you up and take great pains to bring you back once more to Syracuse. Take any of your things you want. We will keep the rest for you also."

At this Callirhoe smiled to herself, greatly troubled though she was, for she realized his utter absurdity. She knew that she was being sold, but in her desire to be rid of the pirates she regarded this sale as a greater good fortune than her former freedom.

"Father," she said, "I thank you for your kind consideration toward me. May Heaven grant to all of you the reward you deserve. But I think it is unlucky to make use of the funeral offerings. Take good care of them all for me. That little ring which I wore as a corpse is enough for me."

Then covering her head she said, "Theron, take me wherever you want. Any place is better than the sea and the tomb."

When he got near to the country house, Theron arranged the following device. Uncovering Callirhoe's head and loosening her hair, he opened the door and told her to go in first. Leonas and all in the room were struck with amazement at her sudden appearance and some of them thought they had seen a goddess. There was, you see, a story that in the fields Aphrodite showed herself to mortals.

In the midst of their astonishment, Theron, who followed after her, approached Leonas and said, "Stand up and get ready to take the girl. She is the one you want to buy."

Joy and amazement on the part of all followed upon his words. Sending Callirhoe off to bed in the finest room in the house, they allowed her to rest, since she was badly in need of recovering from her grief, weariness, and anxiety.

Theron then took Leonas by the hand and said, "My part of the bargain has been faithfully carried out. You may take the girl right now—after all you are a friend of mine—and go to the city and get your title to her registered, and then you can pay me any price you want."

But Leonas, wishing to return the compliment, said, "Not at all. I will trust you with the money now before registering the title,"—and he wanted to establish his prior claim at once, in fear that the other would change his mind, because he knew there would be many eager purchasers in the city.

So he produced a thousand pieces of silver and tried to make Theron take them. Theron, with an affectation of indifference, accepted them. But when

Leonas tried to detain him for dinner (the hour being now late) he said, "I want to sail up to the city this evening, but we will meet each other tomorrow at the harbor."

With this agreement they parted, and Theron went to his ship and gave orders to hoist the anchors and to put out to sea as quickly as possible before they were found out.

Thus while they made their escape, borne along by the breeze, Callirhoe, now left alone, was free to bewail her fate.

"Behold," she said, "yet another tomb more lonely than the first, in which Theron has enclosed me! There my father and mother might have come to see me and Chaereas might have poured forth his tribute of tears. Even in death, I should have thrilled to that. But what friend have I here to call on? Cruel Fortune, hast thou not yet had thy fill of my troubles throughout land and sea? First thou didst make my lover to be my murderer. Chaereas, who never had struck even a slave, launched a mortal blow at me, who loved him. Then thou didst surrender me to the hands of tomb-robbers and didst bring me forth from the tomb to the sea and didst set over me sea-robbers more awful than the very waves. It was for this that I was given the beauty which men acclaim, that Theron, a pirate, might win a great price for me! I have been sold in a lonely place and was not even brought to the city as any other slave might be, for it was thy fear, O Fortune, that if any saw me, they might judge me noble born. That is why I have been handed over like a mere chattel to I know not whom, whether Greeks or barbarians or pirates once again."

As she beat her breast with her hand, she saw on her ring the image of Chaereas, and kissing it, she said, "Chaereas, now truly I am lost to you, parted from you by this mighty deep. You are repenting in grief as you sit by the empty tomb, bearing witness after my death to my innocence, while I, the daughter of Hermocrates, your wife, today have been sold to a master!"

As she thus lamented, sleep gradually came upon her.

BOOK II

BOOK II

EONAS ordered his steward Phocas to take good care of the girl, and while it was still dark, started out by himself to Miletus. He was eager to report to his master the good news about his recent purchase, thinking thus to afford him considerable comfort for his sorrow. He found Dionysius still on his couch. Distraught with grief, he refused for the most part even to appear in public, though the state needed his services, and spent his time in his room as though his wife were still by his side.

On seeing Leonas he said to him, "This is the one night since the death of my poor wife that I have rested comfortably. In fact I saw her distinctly, now grown more stately and beautiful than ever, and she was with me as plain as day. And I thought that it was the beginning of our honeymoon and I was bringing her home as my bride from my estate near the sea, and you were chanting the wedding hymn."

In the midst of his account, Leonas cried out, "Master, you are as lucky now you are awake as you were in your dream. You are now going to hear the facts of what you have seen;" and so he began his story.

"A dealer who had a very beautiful girl for sale approached me. Because of the custom officials he had anchored his boat outside the city limits down near your property. I made an agreement with him and went out to our country place. There we struck a bargain with each other, and practically completed the transaction. In fact, I gave him a thousand pieces of silver, but the title must be properly registered here."

Dionysius was pleased to hear of the beauty of the girl, for he was a true admirer of women, but he was distressed to hear that she was a slave. Being a man of royal blood and pre-eminent in rank and education over all Ionia, he disdained an alliance with a slave.

"Leonas," he said, "it is impossible for a person to be truly beautiful who is not of free birth. Haven't you heard the poets say that beautiful persons are the children of the gods, and hence, by still greater necessity, the children of noblemen? She took your fancy because she was in a lonely place and you compared her with the country women. However, since you have bought her, go to the market place, and Adrastus, who has great knowledge of the law, will arrange the matter of the title."

Leonas was delighted at this incredulity of his, because the unexpected outcome would astonish his master all the more. But though he went down along all the harbors of Miletus and past the money-changers' tables and throughout all the city, he could not find Theron anywhere. He asked questions of dealers and of ferrymen, but no one knew him. Thereupon, greatly embarrassed, he took a small rowboat and rowed down to the beach and went on from there to the farm. But, of course, it was impossible to find his man, since he was already far at sea. So slowly and reluctantly he went back to his master.

Dionysius, seeing his gloomy face, asked what the matter was, and he replied, "Master, I have thrown away your thousand pieces of silver."

"This experience will make you more careful in the future," said Dionysius. "At any rate, what did happen? Your newly bought slave did not run away, did she?"

"No, not she, but the man that sold her did," he said.

"Then he was a kidnapper and that is the reason why he sold you someone else's slave in a lonely place. Where did he say the girl came from?"

"From Sybaris in Italy, sold by her mistress because of jealousy."

"Find out whether there are any people from Sybaris in town. Meanwhile leave the girl there."

Thereupon Leonas went off much troubled because the business had not turned out happily for him. However, he waited for an opportunity to persuade his master to come out to his estate, since his sole remaining hope lay in having him see the girl.

The country women came to visit Callirhoe and at once began to flatter her as their mistress. Plangon, the wife of the overseer and a shrewd sort of creature, said to her, "My child, of course you are longing for your own people, but consider that there are others here too who are your people. Dionysius, our master, is a good and kindly man. It is your good fortune that God has brought you to a good home. You can live here as though in your native land. Now wash away the grime from your long voyage. Here are attendants for you."

Plangon brought her to the bath, reluctant and unwilling as she was. When she entered, the maids anointed her and dried her carefully. While she was still clothed, they marveled at the heavenly beauty of her face. But when she was undressed, they were still more astounded, for they seemed to see in her whole body the beauty of her face. Her skin gleamed white with a refulgence like glistening marble, but her flesh was so delicate that one would fear that even a touch of the finger might produce a serious wound. Softly they whispered to each other, "Our former mistress was famous for her beauty, but she would have seemed to be the servant of this girl."

Their praise troubled Callirhoe and she was not without forebodings of what the future would bring.

When she had been bathed and they were fastening up her hair, they brought her clean clothing. She declared that this was not suitable for one who had just been bought.

"Give me the garment of a slave," she said, "for you are better than I."

So she put on just an ordinary dress, and yet even this was most becoming to her and seemed luxurious in the reflection of her beauty.

When the women had eaten their morning meal, Plangon said to Callirhoe, "Come to Aphrodite's shrine and offer up a prayer for yourself. The goddess makes her appearance here, and not only our neighbors, but people from the city, come here to sacrifice to her. She is especially attentive to Dionysius, and he never fails to stop at her shrine."

They then told of the apparitions of the goddess, and one of the country women said, "Mistress, when you see Aphrodite you will think you are looking at an image of yourself."

When Callirhoe heard this, her eyes filled with tears, and she said to herself, "How unfortunate I am! Here too is the goddess Aphrodite, the cause of all my woes. But I will go over there, for there are many matters with which I want to reproach her."

The temple was near the country house, down by the main thoroughfare. Callirhoe bowed reverently before Aphrodite and clinging to her feet, she said, "Thou first didst show Chaereas to me, but thou hast not preserved the happy union in which thou didst unite us; and yet we continued to pay thee honor! But since thou hast so willed it, I seek one boon of thee. Grant that I never please the eye of any man again, but Chaereas!"

Aphrodite refused this prayer, for she is the mother of Love and she was laying her plans for still another marriage, though she had no intention of keeping that unbroken, either.

Thus Callirhoe, freed from pirates and the perils of the sea, regained her usual beauty and to the marveling eyes of the country folk she seemed to grow more lovely every day.

Leonas, finding an appropriate occasion, addressed Dionysius in these words, "Master, it is now a long time since you have been down to our place by the shore, and matters there require your presence. You must inspect the herds and the crops. The harvest is close at hand. Enjoy also the luxury of the houses which we built there at your command. Then, too, you will bear your grief more easily there, when you are distracted by the pleasures and responsibilities of the country. If there is any herdsman or shepherd of whom you approve, you can give him this newly purchased girl."

Dionysius was pleased at this, and set the date for their departure. When the word had been given, the mule-drivers prepared their wagons, the grooms made ready their horses, the sailors their ferryboats. Friends were invited to join them on the journey, including a large number of freedmen, for the nature of Dionysius was inclined to magnificence. When all was ready, he ordered the equipage and most of the men to cross over by sea and the wagons to follow after him when he himself had gone on ahead, since a formal procession was not seemly for a man in mourning. At earliest dawn, before most men could notice him, he and four companions, of whom one was Leonas, mounted their horses.

And so Dionysius was riding out to the country. Callirhoe meantime, having seen a vision of Aphrodite during the night, wished once more to pay homage to her. She was standing there in prayer when Dionysius jumped down from his horse and entered the temple ahead of the others. Hearing the sound of footsteps, Callirhoe turned about to face him. At the sight of her Dionysius cried, "Aphrodite, be gracious to me, and may thy living presence bless me!"

Just as he was falling to the ground, Leonas caught him and said, "Master, this is the newly bought slave. Do not be disturbed. And you, woman, come to meet your master."

And so Callirhoe bowed her head at the name of "master" and shed a flood of tears, learning at length the bitter lesson of lost freedom.

But Dionysius struck Leonas and said, "Blasphemer, do you address the gods as though they were men? Do you dare call her a purchased slave? No wonder then you could not find the man who sold her. Have you not even heard Homer who tells us, 'Yea and the gods, in the likeness of strangers from far countries, behold the violence and the righteousness of men?'"

Then Callirhoe spoke. "Stop ridiculing me," she said, "and calling me a goddess, when I am not even a happy mortal."

As she spoke, her voice sounded to Dionysius like that of a goddess, for it had a musical tone and, as it were, reproduced the sound of a lyre. In great confusion, therefore, and prevented by his embarrassment from saying more, he went away to the house, now flaming with love.

Not long afterwards the equipage arrived from the city, and the story of what had happened quickly spread abroad. All were then eager to see the girl, though they all pretended that they were doing reverence to Aphrodite. In her modest fear of the crowd, Callirhoe did not know what to do. Everything was strange to her and she could not see even her familiar Plangon, since the latter was busy preparing the reception of her master. As the hour advanced and no one came to the country house, but all stood there as though under a magic spell, Leonas realized what had happened and, coming to the temple precinct, led Callirhoe away. Then you could see that royalty comes by birth, as with the queen bee of the swarm, for they all followed after her of their own accord as though she had been elected by her beauty to be their queen.

Thus she went off to her usual room, while Dionysius, though wounded in heart, tried to conceal his hurt, as you might expect of a well-disciplined person who makes particular claim to manliness. Not wishing to appear contemptible in the eyes of his servants, nor childish before his friends, he grimly held himself in hand throughout the whole evening, thinking thus to avoid detection, but actually betraying himself the more by his very silence. Selecting a portion of his evening meal, he said, "Have someone take this to our guest, but do not say it is from her master, but from Dionysius."

He continued the drinking as long as possible since he knew that he would not be able to sleep, and so he wished to keep vigil with his friends. But when the night had far advanced and he had dismissed the company, he still could get no sleep, but his whole soul was in the shrine of Aphrodite, and he recalled every detail; her face, her hair, how she had turned to him, how she had looked at him, her voice, her dress, her words; even her tears excited him. Then you could observe a struggle between reason and passion, for although sunk deep in the waves of desire, yet like a man of noble nature he tried hard to bear up, and rising, as it were, from the surge, he said to himself, "Are you not ashamed, Dionysius, the leader of Ionia in excellence and high reputation, a man whom governors, kings, and city-states admire,—are you not ashamed to suffer the torments of a mere boy? You fall in love at first sight, and that too while still in mourning and before you have paid due respect to the spirit of your poor wife. Is this why you came to the country, to celebrate a new marriage still clothed in black—and that too with a slave girl who may even belong to another man? Why, you do not have even the legal title to her!"

But Love eagerly came to attack his best intentions and considered his self-restraint outrageous, and for that reason inflamed all the more a loving heart which sought to play the philosopher.

When he could no longer endure this self-communion, he sent for Leonas, who on being summoned, well understood the reason. However, he pretended to be ignorant and, as though startled, he said, "Why are you so sleepless, master? Can it be that sorrow for her who is dead has again overcome you?"

"Sorrow, yes, and for a woman," said Dionysius, "but not for her who is dead. Because of your kindness and your loyalty I have no secrets from you. Leonas, I am utterly ruined and you are the cause of my troubles. You have brought a firebrand into my house, or rather, into my heart. The very mystery which surrounds this woman worries me. You tell me a fairy story about some fly-by-night dealer, and you do not know who he is, nor where he came from, nor where he has gone again. What man who owned beauty such as this would sell her in a lonely place and take a thousand pieces of silver for one who is worth the treasure of a king? What divine power has deceived you? Come now, pay attention and recall what happened. What man did you see? To whom did you speak? Tell me the truth. You did not see any boat!"

25

"No, master, I did not see it, but I heard about it."

"That is just what I thought. It was some nymph of the mountains or from the sea who made her appearance. On occasions fate compels even divinities to seek conversation with men. So the poets and historians tell us."

Thus Dionysius took pleasure in trying to persuade himself into exalting the girl to a company more august than that of mortals.

Leonas, desiring to please his master, said, "Master, let us not concern ourselves as to who she is. I will bring her to you if you wish, so do not nurse your grief, as though you lacked the power to compel her love."

"That I cannot do," said Dionysius, "until I learn who the girl is and where she came from. So, in the morning let us seek the truth from her. To avoid any suspicion of improper constraint, I will not summon her here, but our interview shall be in the temple of Aphrodite, where I first saw her."

So they agreed, and on the following day Dionysius took with him some friends and freedmen and the most trustworthy of his slaves, so as to have witnesses also, and came to the temple precinct. He had dressed himself with some care and had added some slight adornment to his person, in the prospect of conversing with the girl he loved. He was, moreover, naturally handsome and tall and extremely dignified in appearance.

Leonas, taking along Plangon and with her the maids to whom Callirhoe was accustomed, approached her and said, "Dionysius is a most upright and law-abiding gentleman. So come into the temple, lady, and tell him truthfully who you really are, and you shall not fail to receive any lawful aid. Just speak with him simply and do not conceal any of the truth. This will arouse his kindly feelings toward you still more."

So Callirhoe advanced unwillingly and yet with some confidence because their interview was to take place in the temple. When she came, they all admired her still more, and indeed Dionysius was speechless with amazement.

After a prolonged silence, at length he managed to say, "My dear, you know all about me. I am Dionysius, first among the men in Miletus and probably in all Ionia, with a reputation for piety and kindliness. It is only right for you also to tell us the truth about yourself. Those who sold you said that you were from Sybaris and had been sold from that place by your mistress because of her jealousy."

Callirhoe blushed, and lowering her head she said softly, "This is now the first time I have ever been sold. I have never seen the city of Sybaris."

"I told you that she was not a slave," said Dionysius with a look toward Leonas, "and I will guarantee that she is of noble birth besides. Tell me everything, my dear—first of all, your name."

"Callirhoe," she said, and the very name delighted Dionysius. For the rest, however, she remained silent, and when he kept eagerly asking her, she said, "Master, I beg you, allow me to remain silent concerning my past. All that has gone before is dream and story. I am now what I have become, an alien and a slave!"

As she said this, she tried to conceal her agitation, but the tears coursed down her cheeks. Dionysius, too, was moved to tears and all that stood about him. One might have expected Aphrodite herself to have shared their gloom. But Dionysius persisted still more in his curiosity and said, "This is the first favor I ask of you. Tell me your story, Callirhoe; you will not be talking to a stranger, for there exists a natural kinship of character, too. Do not be afraid even if you have committed some dreadful crime."

Callirhoe grew very angry at this and said, "Do not insult me! There is no crime upon my conscience. But since my past history is so much more worthy of respect than my present lot, I do not want to appear boastful, nor to tell a story which those who do not know me would not believe, for my early life does not square with my present case."

Dionysius was astonished at the pride of the girl and said, "I already understand you, even if you say no more. Yet tell us about it. Nothing which you may say about yourself can do justice to the nobility which our eyes behold. Any story of splendor is of slight account compared with yourself."

And so with reluctance she began to tell about herself.

"I am the daughter of Hermocrates, the general of Syracuse. When I had become unconscious as the result of a sudden blow, my parents put me in the tomb with a costly funeral. Tomb-robbers opened the tomb. They found me once more recovering my breath. They brought me here and in a deserted place Theron handed me over to Leonas."—In saying all this she omitted nothing but Chaereas' name.—"But I beg you, Dionysius, since you are a Greek and belong to a civilized city and have your share of refinement, do not be like those tomb-robbers and keep me from my fatherland and kinsmen. To a man of your wealth it is a small thing to rescue one person. You shall not lose my purchase money if you give me back to my father. Hermocrates is not ungrateful. We all admire Alcinoüs and love him because he sent back a suppliant to his native land. I, too, am your suppliant. Save me, an orphan and a prisoner! But if I cannot live as befits my birth, I choose to die as a free woman."

On hearing this, Dionysius wept, ostensibly for Callirhoe, actually for himself, for he saw that he had failed in his love.

"Take courage, Callirhoe," he said, "and keep a stout heart. You shall not fail to obtain what you ask. I call Aphrodite here to witness. But meantime you shall receive from us the treatment which befits a lady rather than a slave."

So she went away convinced that she could suffer no evil against her will, but Dionysius returned sorrowfully to his own house. Then calling in Leonas privately he said, "At every point I am unlucky and the god of love despises me. I buried my wife, and then the girl we have just bought avoids me. I had hoped that she

27

was Aphrodite's gift to me, and I imagined that my life would be happier than that of Menelaus, the husband of Helen of Sparta, for really I do not believe that Helen was as beautiful as she is. But besides this she also has the power of convincing speech. Life is over for me. On the same day on which Callirhoe is taken away, I shall depart from life."

At this Leonas exclaimed, "Not so, master! Do not call down a curse upon yourself. You are her lord and you have authority over her so that if she wills or not, she must do what you think best. I bought her, you know, for a thousand pieces of silver."

"What, you villain! You bought a noble-born girl? Have you never heard of Hermocrates, the general of all Sicily, a man so highly distinguished that the king of Persia admires and loves him? Why, every year he sends him presents for having beaten Persia's enemies, the Athenians. Am I to become a tyrant over a free-born person? Shall I, Dionysius, who have a reputation for discretion and self-restraint, force unwelcome insults on a girl whom not even the pirate Theron could have insulted?"

Such were his words to Leonas. Yet for all that he did not give up hopes of persuading her, for Love is naturally hopeful, and he was confident that he could realize his desire by his attentions to her.

And so calling Plangon he said, "You have already given me sufficient proof of your careful service. Now I entrust you with the greatest and the most valued of my possessions, the stranger girl. I want her to lack nothing, but rather to enjoy every luxury. Take her as your mistress. Care for her, adorn her, and make her friendly to me. Praise me often in her presence. You know the kind of thing to say. Be careful not to call me her master."

Plangon well understood this command, for she was a versatile creature, and unobtrusively catching his purpose in this matter, she hastened to accomplish it. Accordingly she came to visit Callirhoe, but did not inform her that she had received orders to care for her. Instead she sought to demonstrate her own personal interest in her, and desired to gain her confidence as her ally.

And then the following incident took place. Dionysius was prolonging his stay in the country, now on one pretext and now on another. The actual truth was, that he was neither able to part from Callirhoe nor yet willing to bring her back with him, for if she were once seen, she was sure to become celebrated and her beauty would then enthrall all Ionia and her fame would mount even as far as to the Great King.

During his stay as he was making a rather minute investigation of his property, he uttered some sort of criticism of the conduct of the steward, Phocas. Now this criticism did not extend very far, but was merely a matter of words. Yet

Plangon discovered her opportunity in this and in great fear she ran in to Calli-rhoe, tearing her hair. Grasping her by the knees, she said, "Mistress, I beg you, save us! Dionysius is angry with my husband. His nature is to be as severe when angry as he is ordinarily kind. No one can save us except you alone. Dionysius will gladly grant you this first favor if you ask him."

Callirhoe hesitated to go to him, but when Plangon kept begging and beseech-ing her, she could not refuse, being as she was under previous obligations to her for her kindness. And so in order not to seem ungrateful, she said, "I, too, am a slave and have not the right to speak freely, but if you believe that I can do any-thing, such as I am, I am ready to join in your appeals. I only hope we may succeed!"

When they arrived, Plangon told the slave at the door to announce to his master that Callirhoe was there. Now it so happened that Dionysius was lying prostrate with grief, and his body had wasted away. On hearing that Callirhoe had come, he could not speak, and a mist spread over his eyes at the unexpected news. Recovering himself with difficulty, he said, "Have her come in."

So Callirhoe, taking her stand near him, at first bowed her head and blushed deeply. Then with reluctance she spoke.

"I owe a debt of gratitude to Plangon here, for she loves me as her daughter. I beg you, master, do not be angry with her husband, but be so kind as to set him free."

Though she wished to say more, she could not. Dionysius saw through Plan-gon's scheme and said, "I am indeed angry, and no other human being could have saved Phocas and Plangon from ruin after committing such a crime. Yet I am glad to forgive them for your sake. I want you two to know that it is for Callirhoe's sake that you have been saved."

Plangon fell on her knees before him, but Dionysius said "Kneel before Cal-lirhoe; it is she who has saved you."

When Plangon saw Callirhoe's great delight and pleasure at this concession, she said to her, "Then you must express our thanks to Dionysius," and at the same time she pushed her forward. Somehow or other, she stumbled and fell close by the right hand of Dionysius, and he, disdaining merely to give her his hand, drew her to him and kissed her. Then he quickly let her go to avoid any suspicion of premeditation.

The women then went away, but that kiss sank deep into Dionysius' heart like a poison and he was no longer able to see or hear. He was completely taken by storm, and could find no remedy for his love. He could not offer her gifts, since he had observed the girl's proud spirit; he could not use threats or violence, since he was sure that she would choose to die rather than submit to force.

Thus realizing that Plangon was his only resource, he sent for her and said, "The first steps have been well managed. I am grateful to you for that kiss; it is

29

either my salvation or my ruin. So now look for some way to get the better of her as woman to woman. You have me as your ally. Know that freedom is the prize which I set before you and, what I am sure is much dearer to you than freedom, the very life of Dionysius."

Having received her orders, Plangon brought to bear all her experience and skill, but Callirhoe proved completely invincible and remained faithful to Chaereas alone. Yet she was overcome by the stratagems of Fortune, against whom alone human reason has no power. She is a divinity who loves opposition, and there is nothing which may not be expected from her. So on this occasion too she brought about a situation that was astonishing, and even incredible. The way in which she did it is worth hearing.

Fortune had laid her plans to compromise the honor of the girl. At the first consummation of their wedding, Chaereas and Callirhoe had experienced a mutual eagerness each to enjoy the other, and the equal ardor of their passion had rendered their union not without result. Thus shortly before the accident the girl had become pregnant, but, because of the dangers and miseries which followed, she did not immediately realize her condition. At the beginning of the third month, however, her form began to change. Plangon, who was already experienced in feminine matters, recognized the truth on seeing her in the bath. At first she said nothing because of the presence of the crowd of servants, but in the evening when they were at leisure, she sat down beside her on the couch and said, "My daughter, you must realize that you are with child."

Callirhoe burst into tears and cries of grief. Tearing her hair, she exclaimed, "This too, O Fortune, thou hast added to my woes, to become the mother of a slave!" Then, striking her body, she said, "Wretched child, even before your birth you have been in the tomb, and have been given into the hands of pirates! To what manner of life shall you be born? With what hopes for the future can I bear you, a fatherless and homeless slave? You had better die before your birth." But Plangon held fast her hands, promising her that on the next day she would provide an easier means of abortion.

When the two women were alone by themselves, each pursued her own line of reasoning. Plangon thought, "Here is a splendid chance to realize your master's desires. You have the unborn child as your ally. You have found a support to your arguments. Mother love will overcome her womanly modesty." Thus she put together a plausible course of action.

Callirhoe, on the other hand, planned to destroy the child and said to herself, "Am I to allow a descendant of Hermocrates to be born a slave, and shall I bring into the world a child whose father no one knows? Perhaps some malicious people will say, 'Callirhoe conceived the child among the pirates'. It is enough for me alone to suffer. It is no kindness to you, my child, that you should enter into a life of wretchedness from which you must then take flight, even if brought to birth. Go now in freedom, untouched by misery! May you never hear the stories told about your mother!"

Then again she changed her mind, and a sort of pity for the unborn child overcame her. "Are you planning to kill your child?" she said. "Is there a Jason who is brutally insulting you, that you should consider the revenge of a Medea? Why, you will seem even more cruel than the savage Scythian, for she considered her husband as her enemy, while you wish to kill the child of Chaereas and thus leave behind not even a remembrance of our famous marriage. What if it should be a boy? What if he should be like his father? What if he should be happier than I? Are you, his mother, going to kill him when he has been saved from the tomb and from pirates? Think of all the gods and kings of whom we hear, who had sons that were born in slavery and later regained the rank of their fathers, like Zethus and Amphion and Cyrus! My child, some day you too shall sail back to Sicily. You shall seek out your father and grandfather and tell them your mother's story. A fleet shall sail from there to come to my aid. You, my child, shall restore your parents to each other."

While she was thus reasoning with herself throughout all the night, sleep came over her for a little while. A phantom of Chaereas stood before her, resembling him in every respect, "in stature, and fair eyes, and voice, and the raiment of his body was the same," as Homer says. As he stood there, he said, "My wife, I intrust our son to you."

He wanted to say still more, when Callirhoe started up from sleep, eager to embrace him. In the belief, therefore, that her husband had counseled her, she determined to bring up the child.

On the following day when Plangon came, she explained her intention to her. But Plangon did not fail to note the weakness of her plan. "My dear," she said, "it is quite impossible to bring up the baby here with us. Our master is in love with you, and while his respect for you and his own good sense will prevent him from forcing you against your will, still his jealousy will not permit you to rear the child, since he considers it an affront that you hold your absent husband so dear and look with disdain upon himself in his very presence. It seems much better to me for the child to die before, rather than after, its birth. In that way you will profit by escaping unnecessary pain as well as a fruitless pregnancy. It is because of my affection for you that I give you this honest counsel."

Callirhoe listened with heavy heart, and falling on her knees she begged her to discover some means of rearing the child. Plangon, however, refused repeatedly and then postponed her answer for two or three days.

Then, when she had roused Callirhoe to more ardent supplications and thus had increased her own prestige, she first bound her by oath to tell no one of her plan. Thereupon, contracting her brows and rubbing her hands, she said, "My girl, great accomplishments are brought about by great thought. Now I am going to betray my master because of my affection for you. You must realize that one of two things is necessary, either that the child be utterly destroyed or that he be born the wealthiest of Ionians and the heir of a most glorious house. Yes, he shall make you, his mother, happy too. Choose now which you wish."

"Who is so foolish," she said, "as to choose child-murder in place of happiness? However, I think what you say is impossible and incredible, so explain it more clearly."

So Plangon asked, "How long do you think you have been with child?"

"Two months," she said.

"Then the time is right to help us. You can make it appear that you are bearing a seven-months child to Dionysius."

At this Callirhoe cried out in protest, "I would rather have the child die!"

"An excellent plan, my girl," Plangon replied ironically, "to prefer an abortion. Let us do it that way. It is less dangerous than to deceive our master. Cut away completely all remembrance of your noble birth. Let no hope remain of returning home. Adapt yourself to your present fate and really become a slave!"

Callirhoe was quite unsuspicious of Plangon's advice, since she was a high-bred young girl and inexperienced in the tricks of slaves. But the more Plangon urged her to destroy the child, the greater became her pity for it, and she said, "Give me time to consider. My decision is on matters of the highest importance, either my honor or the life of my child."

Plangon once more expressed her approval because she made neither choice hastily, saying, "An inclination either way is justifiable. In the one case it involves the faithfulness of a wife, and in the other the love of a mother. However, there is no time for long delay. By tomorrow certainly you must choose one or the other, before your condition becomes known."

So they agreed and parted from each other.

Going up to her chamber and shutting the door, Callirhoe held the image of Chaereas beneath her heart and said, "Behold, we are three—husband, wife, and child! Let us plan together what is best for us all. I first shall reveal my purpose. I wish to die as the wife of Chaereas alone. This is dearer to me than parents, home-land, and child—not to have experience of another husband.

"But you, my child, what do you choose for yourself? Death by drugs before seeing the sun, and to be cast away together with your mother, and perhaps not even to be thought worthy of a tomb? Or rather to live and to have two fathers, one the leader of Sicily, the other of Ionia? But when you have become a man, you will easily be recognized by your relatives, for I am sure that I shall bear you in the likeness of your father. And you shall sail home in splendor on a Milesian war-vessel, and Hermocrates shall receive his grandson with joy, since by then he will be able himself to be a general. It is a contrary vote which you cast against me, my child, and you do not permit us to die.

"Let us inquire also of your father. But rather he has already spoken, for he himself stood by my side in a dream and said, 'I intrust our son to you.' I call on you, Chaereas, to bear witness that it is you who make me the bride of Dionysius!"

Thus during all that day and night she was engaged in these reflections and was persuaded to live, not for her own sake but for that of the child.

On the following day, Plangon came back, and first sat down beside her, ex-hibiting a mournful and sympathetic appearance, and both remained silent. After a long time had passed, Plangon inquired, "What have you decided? What shall we do? There is no time for delay."

Callirhoe could not answer immediately because of her grief and confusion, but at length she said, "The child has betrayed me against my will. You may do what you consider best. My only fear is that even if I submit to his passion, Diony-sius may feel contempt for my misfortune and consider me not as his wife but as his mistress, and refuse to rear another man's child. Thus I shall have surrendered my modesty in vain."

While she was still speaking, Plangon interrupted her and said, "I have con-sidered that possibility even before you. I love you now more than I do my master. Therefore though I have faith in the character of Dionysius—for he is a good man —however, I will bind him by an oath, master though he be. All this must be done with proper precautions. As for you, my child, when he takes his oath, believe him. I will go now and bring the proposal to him."

BOOK III

BOOK III

DIONYSIUS, disappointed in his love for Callirhoe, and no longer able to carry on, had determined to starve himself to death and was writing his last will with directions for his burial. In the document he begged Callirhoe to visit him even after he was dead.

Plangon meantime wished to come in to see her master, but was prevented by an attendant who had received orders to admit no one. As they were quarreling before the door, Dionysius heard them and asked who was making the disturbance. When the slave told him that it was Plangon, having no further desire to see any one who would remind him of his passion, he replied, "This is a poor time for her to come! However," he added, "call her in."

So she opened the door and said, "Master, why are you tormenting yourself as though all were lost? Callirhoe invites you to marry her. Put on splendid clothing, offer sacrifice, and take to yourself the bride you love!"

At this unexpected announcement Dionysius suffered a great shock. A dark cloud settled down over his eyes and in his weakened condition he collapsed and presented the appearance of a dead man.

With a loud cry of grief Plangon hastily assembled the servants, and throughout all the house the master was mourned as dead. Even Callirhoe could not refrain from tears on hearing this, for as they were mourning for Dionysius, so she was mourning for her husband.

When at length Dionysius had barely regained consciousness, he said in a weak voice, "Some one of the powers above must be deceiving me and wants to turn me from the way of death which lies before me. Is it a dream, or did I really hear this? Does Callirhoe want to become my wife when she has never wished even to be seen by me?"

"Stop," said Plangon, as she came to his side. "There is no use torturing yourself and refusing to believe in your own happiness. I am not deceiving my master. Callirhoe did send me to be her representative to discuss the wedding."

"Do so, then," said Dionysius, "and tell me about it in her own words. Do not take anything away, do not add anything, but quote her exactly."

" 'I,' she said, 'belong to the first family in Syracuse. I have been the victim of misfortune, but I still maintain my pride. I have been deprived of homeland and parents, and my noble birth is the only thing I have not lost. And so, if Dionysius desires to have me as a mistress for the mere satisfaction of his passion, I will hang myself rather than submit to such slavish outrage. But if he wishes to have me as his legal wife, then for my part I am willing to become a mother, so that the race of Hermocrates may have a successor.

"'Let Dionysius think this over, not by himself and not in haste, but in company with his friends and relatives. Then no one can say to him afterwards, "Do you intend to bring up children born of a slave that you bought, and thus bring shame upon your house?" If he does not wish to become a father, then he need not become my husband.'"

These words excited Dionysius all the more, and he had some slight hope that his love was requited. Stretching his hand toward heaven, he said, "Zeus and Helios, if only I may behold a child born of Callirhoe! Then I shall think myself happier than the Great King. Let us go and see her. Show me the way, my devoted Plangon."

When he had hastened to the upper chamber, his first impulse was to fall at Callirhoe's knees. However, he restrained himself and took his seat with dignity.

"I have come, my dear," he said, "to thank you for saving my life. I did not intend to force you against your will, yet if I had not won you, I was determined to die. I have been restored to life because of you. Yet, though I feel ever so grateful to you, I have a complaint to make. You did not believe that I would consider you my wife, 'for the begetting of children' according to the laws of the Greeks. If I were not in love with you, I should not have prayed for that sort of marriage. But apparently you judged me so insane as to regard a noble-born girl as a slave, and a descendant of Hermocrates as unworthy to be my son. 'Think it over carefully,' you say. I have already done so. Do you fear my friends—you who are the dearest of them all? Who shall dare to call any child of mine unworthy, when he has a grandfather even greater than his father?"

Saying this with tears in his eyes, he approached her, and she, blushing, gently kissed him and said, "I believe you, Dionysius, but I cannot trust Fortune. You see, she has caused my downfall before under even better circumstances and I am afraid that she is not yet done with me. Therefore, though you are a good and honorable man, swear by the powers of Heaven—not on your own account, but for the sake of your fellow citizens and relatives—so that no one may be able thereafter to recommend any unkind treatment of me, since he will know that you have taken your oath. A lonely woman in a strange land is of little account."

"What gods do you want me to swear by?" he said. "I am ready to mount even into Heaven, if that were possible, to swear with my hand upon Zeus himself."

"Swear," she said, "by the sea that brought me to you and by Aphrodite who showed me to you, and by Eros who brings the bride."

So they agreed and it was done at once.

38

Thus their romance rapidly advanced and suffered no delay to the wedding, for when opportunity is at hand, it is hard to set a limit to passion. Dionysius, though a man of excellent training, was caught by the storm and his heart was overwhelmed. Yet he forced himself to bear up, as it were, from the mighty flood of his passion. He occupied himself, accordingly, with thoughts such as these:

"Am I to marry her here in a lonely place, as though she really were a slave I had bought? No, I am not so ungrateful as to refuse to celebrate my wedding with Callirhoe openly. This is the first point in which I must honor my wife. Then, again, this will bring me security against the future. Rumor is the swiftest of all things. She flits through the air and no way is closed to her. Because of her, no strange thing can remain secret. Already she is hurrying to bring the news to Sicily—'Callirhoe is alive! Tomb-robbers opened the tomb and stole her and she is sold in Miletus.' Presently Syracusan ships will sail here with the general, Hermocrates, demanding back his daughter.

"What am I going to say? 'Theron sold her to me?' But where is Theron? And if they do believe that, shall I tell them the truth, that I am the receiver of stolen goods from a pirate? Dionysius, you had better practice your case. Possibly you will have to plead it before the Great King. If so, it will be best to say, 'I heard that somehow or other a free-born girl was stopping here. With her own consent I married her in the city, openly and in accordance with law.' In this way I shall more easily persuade my father-in-law that I am not unworthy of this marriage. So be patient, my heart, just for a short interval, and then you can enjoy your pleasure in safety all the longer. I shall have a stronger case if it comes to trial, if I am in the position of a husband and not of a master."

After reaching this decision he called Leonas and said, "Go up to the city and get things ready for the wedding in grand style. Have them drive down flocks of sheep, have them bring food and wine by land and sea. I have decided to give a public banquet for all the city."

After giving careful and detailed directions, on the following day he himself made the trip in a chariot, but since he did not want as yet to show Callirhoe to the general public, he told her to take the ferry near evening and to come to his house which was situated on the very edge of the harbor called Docimus, and he commissioned Plangon to take good care of her.

As Callirhoe was about to leave the farm, she first offered another prayer to Aphrodite. She entered the temple and ordered all the others out; then she spoke to the goddess as follows:

"Mistress Aphrodite, ought I to blame thee or be grateful to thee? Thou didst wed me to Chaereas when I was a girl, but now thou dost make me the bride of another man after him. I would never have consented to take oath by thee and thy son, had not this child"— and here she pointed to her body —"betrayed me. I beseech thee," she said, "not for my sake but for his, allow my deceit to remain undetected. Since this child does not have his real father, let people think that he is the son of Dionysius. When he is grown to manhood, he will find his real father, too."

As she walked from the sacred precinct down to the sea, the boatmen were overwhelmed with awe on seeing her, as though Aphrodite herself were coming to embark, and with one accord they hastened to bow low before her. Then so eagerly did they row that the boat sailed into the harbor in less time than it takes to tell.

At early dawn all the city was adorned with garlands. Every man offered sacrifice before his own house as well as in the temples. There were many conjectures as to who the bride might be. Because of the girl's beauty and her unfamiliar appearance, the more humble class of people was persuaded that she was some nymph who had risen from the sea, or that she was a goddess who had come from Dionysius' estate, for such was the gossip of the boatmen. All, however, had but one desire, and that was to see Callirhoe; and the crowd was massed about the temple of Concord where it was the tradition for bridegrooms to receive their brides.

On this occasion, for the first time since the funeral, Callirhoe had herself adorned with all her finery, for hitherto, in her determination to marry but once, she had considered that beauty lay in nobility of fatherland and race. When she had put on her Milesian dress and a bridal wreath, she looked out at the assembled crowd. All of them then shouted, "It is Aphrodite who is the bride!" Beneath her feet they spread purple cloth and roses and violets. As she walked they sprinkled her with perfume. Not a person, young or old, was left inside the houses, nor even within the very harbors. Cramped for space, the crowd climbed up to the roof tiles.

But once more on this day, too, the demon of ill-will indignantly took a hand. Just how, I shall narrate a little later, but first I want to tell what happened in Syracuse during this same time.

The tomb-robbers had carelessly closed the tomb, hurrying as they were in the dark. Chaereas waited for the moment of dawn and came to the tomb, ostensibly to bring wreaths and libations, but really with the purpose of killing himself. He could not bear separation from Callirhoe and considered death the only way to heal his sorrow. When he arrived, he discovered that the stones had been moved and that someone obviously had gone in. He was astonished at this sight and overcome with utter dismay at what had happened.

Rumor swiftly brought this extraordinary news to Syracuse, whereupon they all hurried together to the tomb, but no one dared to go inside until Hermocrates gave the order. A man was sent in and brought out a complete and accurate report. It seemed unbelievable that not even the corpse was lying there. Then Chaereas himself darted in, eager to see Callirhoe once more even though she was dead, but searching the tomb he could find nothing. Many others entered incredulously after him.

A sense of helplessness came over them all, until one man standing in the tomb said, "The funeral offerings have been stolen! This is the work of tomb-robbers. But where is the corpse?"

Many and various were the theories which occupied the crowd. But Chaereas, raising his eyes toward heaven, stretched forth his hands and said, "Which one of the gods is it who has become my rival and has carried Callirhoe away and now holds her by his side, not of her own will, but compelled by a mightier fate? This, then, is why she died so suddenly, that she might not be disfigured with disease! So once Dionysius robbed Theseus of Ariadne and Zeus stole Semele.

"Or can it be that I had a goddess as my wife and did not know it, and she was beyond my human station? But, even so, she should not have disappeared so quickly from the sight of men, however good her excuse. Thetis, too, was a goddess, but she remained with Peleus and bore him a son, while I have been deserted in the very perfection of my love. What is in store for me? What will become of me, poor wretch that I am? Shall I kill myself? With whom then shall I be buried? I once had this consoling hope that if I could no longer share my chamber with Callirhoe, at least I should find a common tomb with her.

"Queen of my heart, listen to my one excuse for living! It is you who compel me to live. I shall search for you over land and sea—yes, if I may, I shall mount even into the sky. Only I beg you, my darling, do not flee from me."

At these words the crowd broke forth into lamentations, and all began to mourn for Callirhoe as though she had just died.

Boats were immediately launched and many shared in the search. Hermocrates himself explored Sicily, and Chaereas, Libya. Some were dispatched to Italy and others were ordered to cross the Ionic Gulf.

However, human resources proved entirely inefficient, and it was Fortune who brought the truth to light—Fortune, without whose aid no work is ever complete, as you may learn from what happened here.

The tomb-robbers, after selling their embarrassing cargo, left Miletus and were making the voyage toward Crete. They had heard that it was a great and prosperous island and there they hoped that the disposal of their wares would be easy. But a violent wind caught them and forced them out into the Ionic Gulf, where they drifted about in lonely waters. Thunder and lightning and prolonged darkness fell upon these villains, and Providence showed them plainly that until now they had had fair sailing only because of Callirhoe. Each time they came near to death, God refused to release them immediately from their terror, but pro-

longed the agony of their shipwreck. The dry land refused to receive such wicked-
ness as theirs and so, as they continued to float long upon the sea, they were
reduced to shortage of provisions, especially of water. Their ill-gotten riches were
of no help to them, and they were dying of thirst in the midst of gold. Thus gradually they came to repent of their crime, and reproached each other with the use-
lessness of it.

Now all the rest were dying of thirst, but Theron even at this juncture proved
himself a villain. He secretly stole some of the water, and thus robbed his fellow
robbers. He thought of course that he had done a very clever thing, but really this
was the work of Providence, reserving him for tortures and crucifixion.

The warship with Chaereas on board fell in with this craft in the course of its
wanderings, and at first they avoided it, thinking it belonged to pirates; but since
it was evidently without a pilot and was riding erratically against the impact of the
waves, someone from the warship shouted, "There's nobody aboard! We needn't
be afraid. Instead let's pull up close and look into this mystery."

The pilot agreed, for Chaereas was in the ship's waist with his head covered
and weeping. When they drew near, at first they hailed the crew; then, when no
one answered, a man from the warship went on board and could see nothing but
gold and corpses. He made his report to his mates. They were delighted and congratulated themselves on finding a treasure-trove at sea.

Hearing the disturbance, Chaereas asked what the trouble was, and, on being
told, wanted to look into this strange business for himself. When he recognized the
funeral offerings, he tore his clothes in grief and in loud, penetrating tones he exclaimed, "My poor Callirhoe, these things belong to you! Here is the wreath which
I put about your head; your father gave you this; and this is from your mother; and
here is your bridal dress. The ship has become your tomb. Yes, I can see your
things, but where are you? Of all the contents of the tomb, your body alone is
missing!"

On hearing this, Theron lay like the dead, and indeed he was half-dead. He
resolved many times not to utter a word or make a motion, for he had a fair idea of
what was to come. Yet man is a life-loving creature and even in utter extremities
he does not lose hope of a change for the better, since the God who created us has
implanted this conceit in the minds of us all to prevent us from taking flight from
the wretchedness of life. Accordingly, being overwhelmed with thirst, he first
gasped forth one word—"Drink!"

When it had been brought to him and he had received every attention, Chaereas sat down beside him and questioned him.

"Who are you? Where are you sailing? Where did these things come from?
What have you done with their rightful owner?"

Theron, like the rascal he was, bethought himself and said, "I am a Cretan
and I am sailing to Ionia. I am looking for my brother in the army there. I was left

behind in Cephallenia by the ship's company when they put out from there in a hurry. I got on board this boat which was conveniently sailing by. We were forced off our course by violent winds into this part of the sea. Then a prolonged calm fell, and we all perished with thirst. I alone was saved because of my piety."

On hearing this, Chaereas gave orders to fasten the craft to the warship until he sailed into the harbor of Syracuse.

But Rumor, naturally swift-moving, on that occasion was in special haste to report these many strange happenings, and arrived home ahead of him. Thus all the Syracusans were running together to the seashore, and emotions of all kinds at once were manifest; men wept, marveled, asked questions, and expressed doubts, for naturally this strange account astounded them.

When Callirhoe's mother saw the funeral offerings of her daughter, she uttered a cry of anguish. "I recognize them all, but you, my child, you alone are missing! A strange sort of tomb-robbers! They have kept safe the clothing and the gold and have stolen away only my daughter!"

The shores and harbors resounded with the beating of breasts. Land and sea were filled with the women's cries. But Hermocrates, a man of high military prestige and practical experience, said, "We must not investigate the matter here, but we must make our inquiry more in accordance with the laws. Let us go to the assembly. Who knows whether we may have need of a jury?"

While the word was yet on his lips, the theater was now filled. In that assembly women too could participate. The citizens sat high on the benches and Chaereas entered first, clothed in black, pale, disheveled, just as he was when he accompanied his wife to the tomb. He did not want to mount upon the platform, but, standing below, at first he wept for a long time and in spite of himself, he could not speak.

The crowd shouted, "Be brave and speak!"

So, scarcely raising his eyes, he said, "This is really no time for a long speech, but rather an occasion of mourning. I speak and indeed live, compelled by one and the same purpose—to find the means of recovering Callirhoe. It was for that reason that I set sail from here, and I do not know whether I have made a success or a failure of my voyage. We saw a boat drifting about in fair weather, laboring under a tempest of its own making, and sinking in a calm. Surprised at this, we came nearer, and I thought I was looking at the tomb of my poor wife. Everything that was hers was there, except herself. There were great numbers of dead bodies, but all of strangers. This man was found among them half dead. I restored him to health with every attention and I have kept him to show to you."

Meantime the public slaves brought Theron into the theater in chains with the sort of attendance he well deserved. The wheel and the rack and fire and whips followed after him, since Providence was now awarding him the suitable prize for his endeavors.

43

When he had taken his stand among the officials, one of them asked him, "Who are you?"

"Demetrius," he said.

"Where do you come from?"

"Crete," he said.

"What do you know? Tell me."

"On my way to meet my brother in Ionia, I missed the boat, and then I got on board a small craft sailing by. Well, at that time I thought they were traders, but now I know they were tomb-robbers. After a long time at sea all the others died off for want of water, and I was barely saved because never in my life have I done any wicked thing. Men of Syracuse, a city famous for its kindly nature, do not be more cruel to me than thirst and the sea!"

When he said this so mournfully, the hearts of the crowd were struck with pity, and he might have won them over even to the point of receiving aid for his journey, had not his unscrupulous eloquence aroused the indignation of some heavenly avenger of Callirhoe's wrongs, to ensure his still greater punishment. For indeed a most outrageous state of affairs was on the point of ensuing, namely that the one man who had been saved by his impious rascality should persuade the Syracusans that he alone had been saved by his piety.

Then a certain fisherman who sat among the crowd recognized him and said quietly to those that sat beside him, "I have seen this fellow before, roving about our harbor."

This speech was quickly passed on to several others, and someone shouted, "He lies!"

All the people turned around, and the officials ordered the man who had spoken first to come down front. When Theron denied the charge, the fisherman was believed all the more. Immediately they called for the torturers, and whips were applied to the criminal. Yet, though burned and lashed, he held out for a long time and almost succeeded in overcoming the tortures. Nevertheless, for every individual conscience is mighty and truth is all-powerful.

Slowly, then, and with reluctance Theron confessed, and began his story. "I saw the treasure that was being buried and got together my gang. We opened the tomb. We found the corpse come to life. We cleaned out the place and put everything into our boat. We sailed to Miletus and there we sold only the girl and were carrying everything else on to Crete. But we were forced out of our course by the winds into the Ionic Gulf, and what happened to us then you yourselves have seen."

In telling all this, the only thing he failed to mention was the name of Callirhoe's purchaser.

At this account, they were all filled with both joy and grief—joy because Callirhoe was still alive, and grief because she had been sold into slavery. A sentence of death was voted against Theron, but Chaereas begged them not to put him to death for awhile.

"I want him to come," he said, "and point out to me her purchasers. Think of the constraint I am under. I am acting as the advocate of the man who sold my wife!"

But Hermocrates refused to allow this, saying, "It is better to make our search more difficult than to allow the laws to be broken. Men of Syracuse, I beg you, in memory of my services as a general and of my triumphs, show me your gratitude in the case of my daughter. Dispatch an embassy in her behalf. Let us get her back, a free girl."

Before he had finished speaking, the members of the assembly shouted, "Let us all sail!"—and the greater part of the members of the Senate offered themselves as volunteers.

But Hermocrates said, "I thank you all for this honor, but two ambassadors from the assembly and two from the Senate will be sufficient, and Chaereas himself shall sail as the fifth."

So they decided and thus it was decreed, and thereupon he dismissed the assembly. A great proportion of the crowd followed after Theron as he was led away, and in front of Callirhoe's tomb he was impaled upon the cross, and from the cross gazed out upon that sea over which he had carried captive the daughter of Hermocrates whom not even the Athenians had been able to capture.

Now all the others thought best to wait for the season of navigation, and to set sail at the first flush of spring, for then it was still winter and it seemed entirely impossible to cross the Ionic Gulf. But Chaereas, impatient to start because of his love, was quite ready to bundle a raft together, and to project himself upon the sea for the winds to carry along. Moreover, the ambassadors also were unwilling to delay because of the respect they felt for him and especially for Hermocrates, and so they made ready to sail. The Syracusans sent out the expedition at public expense so that this too might contribute to the dignity of the embassy. Accordingly they launched the famous flagship which still bore the standards of their victory.

When the designated day of sailing arrived, the crowd ran in a body toward the harbor, not only men but also women and children, and there were mingled together prayers, tears, groans, words of comfort, terror, courage, resignation, and hope.

Ariston, Chaereas' father, was carried down because of his extreme age and illness. He put his arms about the neck of his son and clinging there, he wept and said, "Only think what it means, my child, to leave me now. I am an old man and nearly dead. I am sure that I shall never see you again. Wait just a few days and let me die in your arms; then bury me and go."

His mother, too, knelt and clung to him, and said, "I beg you, my child, do not leave me here all alone, but put me on the boat. I shall be a light load, but if I am burdensome and in the way, you can throw me over into the sea and thus sail on."

So saying she tore her clothes in grief and extending her breast, she said in the words of Homer, "My child, have regard unto this bosom and pity me if ever I gave thee consolation of my breast."

Chaereas' heart was broken at the appeals of his parents, and he hurled himself from the ship into the sea, wishing to die so as to escape the dreadful choice either of giving up his search for Callirhoe, or of causing pain to his parents. But immediately the sailors jumped in after him and brought him up with difficulty. Then Hermocrates dispersed the crowd and told the pilot to set sail.

But still another rather noble demonstration of friendship took place. For the moment, Polycharmus, Chaereas' comrade, was not to be seen in their midst. As a matter of fact, he had said to his parents, "Chaereas is my friend, to be sure; but not, however, to the point of going to extremes in sharing danger with him. And so until he sails, I shall keep out of sight." But in spite of this, when the boat drew away from the shore, he waved farewell to his parents from the stern, so they could no longer hold him back.

As he went out of the harbor, Chaereas looked off over the deep and prayed, "God of the sea, take me on that same course over which thou didst take Callirhoe. Poseidon, I pray thee that either she may return with us or that I may never come back without her. If I cannot regain my wife, I am willing even to be a slave, if only I am with her."

A favorable breeze wafted the ship on and it ran, as it were, in the very track of Theron's vessel. They came to Ionia in just the same number of days and anchored at the same beach on the estate of Dionysius. Then the others in a state of exhaustion disembarked and hastened to refresh themselves, setting up tents and preparing a feast. Chaereas, however, was strolling about with Polycharmus and said, "How can we find Callirhoe now? I am very much afraid that Theron has lied to us and that the poor girl is dead. Then, too, even if she really has been sold, who knows where? Asia is a broad land."

Meantime in their wanderings they happened upon the shrine of Aphrodite. They therefore determined to pay their respects to the goddess, and Chaereas, hastily assuming the attitude of prayer before her knees, said, "Thou, mistress, didst first show Callirhoe to me at thy festival. Do thou give her back to me now since thou didst grant her to me."

Just then he looked up and saw beside the goddess a golden statue of Callirhoe, an offering of Dionysius. "His knees and heart were unstrung," and he fell with reeling senses. Seeing him, the temple attendant brought water and restored him. Then she said, "Come, my child, don't be alarmed; there are plenty of others, too, whom the goddess has frightened out of their senses. You see, she actually

46

appears in person and distinctly shows herself. However, this is a sign of great good luck. Do you see this golden statue? This girl was once a slave, and Aphrodite has made her the mistress of us all."

"Who is she?" said Chaereas.

"She is the mistress of this whole estate, my child, and the wife of Dionysius, who is first in rank among the Ionians."

On hearing this, Polycharmus, who was himself a man of good sense, would not allow Chaereas to say any more, but taking him by the arm, he led him away, since he did not want it to be discovered who they were, until they had considered the whole matter carefully and had come to a mutual agreement. So Chaereas said nothing in the presence of the temple attendant, and maintained a stubborn silence, except that the tears welled up beyond his control.

But when he had withdrawn some distance, he threw himself upon the ground and exclaimed, "God of the sea, how kind thou art! Why hast thou brought me here in safety? Was it to enjoy a pleasant voyage, and then to see Callirhoe the wife of another? I had never expected that to happen, no, not even after Chaereas' death! Poor fool that I am, what shall I do? I was expecting to get you back from some master and I was confident that I could win over the man who bought you with ransom money. But now I have found you wealthy, perhaps even a queen. How much happier I should be, if I had found you a beggar! Shall I go to Dionysius and say, 'Give back your wife to me?' Who can say that to a husband? Why, supposing I meet you, I cannot even come up to you, or greet you as my fellow citizen, the commonest of courtesies. Perhaps I shall even be in danger of death as the adulterer of my own wife!" As he was thus lamenting, Polycharmus tried to comfort him.

Meantime Phocas, Dionysius' overseer, had caught sight of the war vessel, and had become somewhat alarmed. By fraternizing with one of the crew, he learned the truth from him as to their identity, their port of origin, and the purpose of their voyage. He realized then that the arrival of this vessel was fraught with utter ruin for Dionysius, who could not live if separated from Callirhoe, and so, as a loyal servant, he was eager to forestall the danger and to quench the spark of an encounter which, though not great nor of general concern, did, however, affect the house of his master Dionysius exclusively.

For this reason he rode off to a certain garrison of barbarian soldiers and reported that an enemy ship lay hidden at anchor, possibly with the purpose of spying, possibly also intending piracy, and that it was in the interests of the king to seize hold of it before it did any harm. He convinced the barbarians and brought them down in marching order. At midnight they fell upon the ship, and threw firebrands upon it and so set it aflame. They captured the crew alive and put them all in chains and brought them back to the garrison. When it came to a division of the prisoners, Chaereas and Polycharmus begged to be sold to the same master.

Accordingly the man who got them sold them into Caria and there, dragging stout chains on their feet, they labored on the estate of Mithridates.

Now Callirhoe had a dream in which Chaereas appeared before her, bound in chains and eager to approach her, but unable to do so. In her sleep she distinctly cried out aloud, "Chaereas, come to me."

That was the first time that Dionysius had heard the name of Chaereas, and to her great confusion he asked the girl, "Who is this man you called?"

Her tears betrayed her and she could not repress her grief, but gave free rein to her feelings.

"He is a poor, unhappy creature," she said; "the man I married as a girl. Even in the dream he was not happy; I could see that he was bound in chains. My poor husband, you must have died while searching for me, since to dream of chains means death. And meantime I am living in luxury and lie upon a gold-wrought couch with another man! But it will not be long before I come to you. Though in life we could not enjoy each other's company, yet in death we shall possess each other."

On hearing these words, Dionysius was the prey of conflicting thoughts. He was, to be sure, seized with jealousy because she loved Chaereas even when dead, and also he was afraid that she might kill herself. On the other hand, he felt confident that since the girl believed that her first husband had died, she surely would not desert Dionysius now that Chaereas was no more. And so he comforted her as much as he could and kept watch on her for several days to see that she did no harm to herself.

As for Callirhoe, her grief was distracted by the hope that perhaps after all Chaereas was still living and the dream had been false. Still more important was her child. In the seventh month after the wedding she had given birth to a son, to all appearances the child of Dionysius, but really that of Chaereas. The city celebrated a great festival and embassies arrived from everywhere to join in congratulating the people of Miletus on the fact that the house of Dionysius had received an heir. Dionysius in his joy yielded to his wife in all matters and made her the mistress of his house. He filled the temples with offerings and throughout the city provided sacrificial feasts to all.

Callirhoe was greatly worried for fear that her secret would be betrayed, and so, since Plangon alone shared her knowledge that she was already pregnant when she came to Dionysius, she demanded that she should be given her freedom, hoping thus to secure her loyalty not only through mere inclination but also through gratitude for her improved fortune.

"I am glad," said Dionysius, "to repay Plangon for the service she did for my love, but it will be unjust if we reward the servant and do not pay our thanks to Aphrodite at whose shrine we first saw each other."

"I am even more eager than you to do that," said Callirhoe, "since I have greater cause to thank her. Just now, however, I am confined to my bed. Let us wait for a few days, and then it will be safer for us to go to her shrine in the country."

She quickly recovered from her confinement and became more and more beautiful, since she was no longer a child but had taken on the full bloom of womanhood. When they arrived at the farm, Phocas prepared a magnificent sacrificial banquet, since a large number of people had followed them from town. At the beginning of the main sacrificial rites, Dionysius prayed as follows:

"Mistress Aphrodite, thou art the cause of all my blessings. From thee I have Callirhoe, and from thee I have a son. Through thee I am a husband and a father. Though Callirhoe was enough for me and dearer to me than homeland and parents, yet I love the child because he has made his mother more surely mine. I have in him a pledge of the affection she feels for me. Mistress, I beseech thee, preserve Callirhoe for my sake and preserve my son for Callirhoe's sake."

The crowd that stood about him confirmed his prayer with cries of joy and pelted them both with flowers, some with roses, others with violets, and still others with whole garlands, so that the precinct was filled with flowers.

Dionysius had uttered his prayer in the hearing of all, but Callirhoe wished to speak to Aphrodite by herself. So first she took the child in her arms, and thus presented a most charming sight, the like of which no painter has ever portrayed, nor sculptor fashioned, nor poet described to the present day; for no one of them has created an Artemis or an Athena holding a child in her arms. On seeing her, Dionysius wept for very joy and quietly made a sign to ward off jealous fate. She then told Plangon alone to stay with her and sent the others on ahead to the country house.

Then, when they had gone off, she stood close to Aphrodite and holding up her child in her arms, she prayed, "Mistress, for this child I offer thee thanks; for myself I feel no gratitude. If thou hadst preserved Chaereas for me, then I should be grateful for my own sake as well. But at least thou hast granted me this image of my dearest husband, and so hast not taken Chaereas wholly from me. Grant that my son be happier than his parents and like to his grandsire. May he, too, set sail on board a flagship, and may men say of his prowess on the sea, 'Hermocrates' grandson is greater than he'. His grandsire, too, shall be happy to have a successor in his valor, and we, his parents, shall feel that delight even though we are dead. I beseech thee, mistress, from now on be reconciled to me, for my misfortune is great enough. I have died, and been restored to life; I have been kidnapped and taken into exile; I have been sold and made a slave. Yet I consider this second marriage even harder to bear. In return for it all I beg from thee and, through thee, from the other gods one favor: Save my fatherless child!"

Though she wished to say more, her tears prevented her.

After a little time she called the priestess. Obeying her summons, the old woman said, "My child, what are you crying for? Just think of your blessings! Why, even strangers are worshiping you as a goddess now. The other day two fine young men from a coasting vessel stopped here, and one of them came near fainting when he saw your statue, so like a goddess on earth has Aphrodite made you."

Callirhoe's heart was struck by these words, and with staring eyes, as though she had gone mad, she cried, "Who were the strangers? Where did they sail from? What story did they tell you?"

The old woman at first stood speechless with fright, and then haltingly she said, "I only saw them. I heard nothing."

"What sort of men did they look like? Recall their appearance."

The old woman made no clear answer; however, Callirhoe suspected the truth, for people are prone to think that what they really want is so. With a glance toward Plangon she said, "It may be that poor Chaereas has come here in his wanderings. What has happened to him? Let us look for him, but tell no one."

When she came back to Dionysius, she told him only what she had heard from the priestess, fully aware that the restless curiosity so natural to love would lead Dionysius to inquire for himself into what had happened. And this indeed is just what occurred. On acquiring the facts, Dionysius was immediately filled with jealousy, and, while he was far from suspecting Chaereas, he was afraid that some scandalous plot was secretly in progress there at the farm. Indeed, the beauty of his wife induced him to suspect and fear all kinds of things. Not only did he fear the plots of men, but he actually expected that perhaps some divinity would descend from heaven to be his rival.

Therefore he called Phocas and cross-examined him carefully: "Who are these young men and where did they come from? Men of wealth and fine appearance, I suppose? Why were they worshipping my Aphrodite? Who told them about her? Who permitted them to do so?"

Phocas tried to conceal the truth, not so much from fear of Dionysius, but in the knowledge that Callirhoe would ruin him and his whole family if she found out about what had happened. Accordingly he denied that anyone had visited there, but Dionysius failing to appreciate his motives, suspected a still more serious plot was in progress against himself. So in great anger he demanded whips and the wheel of torture for Phocas, and included in his summons not only Phocas but all the people at the farm, convinced that he was ferreting out a matter of adultery.

But Phocas, perceiving the danger of his position, whether he spoke or remained silent, said, "Master, I will tell you the truth and you alone."

Dionysius then sent them all away and said, "Well, here we are alone. Tell me no more lies. Speak the truth, however disgraceful it may be."

"There is nothing disgraceful, master," he said. "I am bringing you really excellent news. And if the beginning is a little ominous, do not be worried or feel hurt on that account. Wait until you hear it all; it comes out nicely for you in the end."

Greatly excited at the promised news, Dionysius hung upon his words, and said, "Don't be so slow! Tell me your story."

So then he began to speak: "A warship sailed in here from Sicily with ambassadors from the Syracusans to demand Callirhoe back from you."

On hearing this, Dionysius fainted, and a blackness spread over his eyes; he had a vision of Chaereas standing before him and dragging Callirhoe from him. So he lay with the appearance and the color of a dead man, and Phocas in turn was reduced to a state of helplessness, since he did not wish to summon anyone for fear of having a witness to his secret. At length he gradually restored his master by saying, "Cheer up. Chaereas is dead. His ship has been destroyed. There is nothing more to fear."

These words put life into Dionysius, and gradually returning to his senses, he inquired carefully about the whole matter. Phocas told him about the sailor who had informed him where the warship came from, and the reason for their sailing, and who the visitors were; he explained also his own device of resorting to the barbarians, the happenings of the night, the fire, the shipwreck, the bloodshed, and the chains.

Then, as it were, Dionysius cleared away the last cloud from his mind and, embracing Phocas he said, "You are my benefactor; you are my true protector and the most faithful guardian of my secrets. It is through you that I possess Callirhoe and my son. I would not, to be sure, have ordered you to kill Chaereas, but since you have done so, I have no fault to find. The crime was that of a loyal servant. But you were careless in this one point; you did not inquire carefully whether Chaereas was among the dead or among the prisoners. You should have looked for his body. Then, you see, he would have gained a burial and I would have had surer grounds for confidence. As it is, I cannot help worrying about my security because of those prisoners, since we do not know where they have been sold."

He instructed Phocas to speak openly of everything else that had happened, but to keep two matters secret: first, the stratagem he had employed, and, second, the fact that some of the men on the warship were still alive. Then with a gloomy expression he came to Callirhoe, and calling together the countrymen of the neighborhood, questioned them in her presence, so that she, on learning what had happened, might then more certainly give up all hope for Chaereas.

So they all came and proceeded to tell what they knew: "Barbarian robbers charging down from somewhere during the night set fire to a Greek warship which on the previous day had anchored near the beach, and by daylight we saw the waters stained with blood and corpses riding on the waves."

On hearing this, Callirhoe tore her clothes with grief, and beating her hands against her eyes and cheeks, she ran back into the house she first had entered when sold as a slave. Dionysius allowed her free expression of her feelings, fearing that his untimely presence might prove offensive. Accordingly he ordered everyone to let her alone; only Plangon was to sit beside her so as to prevent her doing some harm to herself.

Callirhoe, now she had obtained quiet, sat upon the earthen floor and sprinkled dust upon her head; she tore her hair, and began aloud as follows: "Chaereas, it was my prayer to die before you or to die with you. In any case, my death at least must follow yours. What hope is now left to keep me alive? Until now in my misfortune I used to think, 'Some day I shall see Chaereas and I shall tell him all that I have suffered for him, and this will make me dearer to him. What joy will fill his heart when he sees our son!' All this has become useless to me; even the child is now an extra burden, since, to crown my misfortunes, he is now fatherless. Cruel Aphrodite, thou alone didst see Chaereas and didst not show him to me when he came. Thou hast betrayed his fair body to the hands of robbers. Thou didst have no pity on him who for thy sake sailed the sea. Who could offer prayer to such a goddess, when thou hast caused the death of thine own suppliant? On that dreadful night thou gavest no aid, when thou sawest near thee a fair young lover made the victim of murder. Thou hast taken from me my comrade, my countryman, my lover, my darling, my husband! Give him back to me even though he is dead!

"I believe that we were born the most unfortunate of all mankind. What crime had that gallant ship committed that barbarians should have destroyed it by fire, when not even the Athenians had been able to vanquish it? Even now the parents of us both are seated by the seashore longing and waiting for our return, and whenever a ship is seen in the distance they say, 'There comes Chaereas to bring Callirhoe home!' They make ready our wedding chamber and the room is adorned for us who have not even a tomb of our own. O cruel sea! Thou hast brought Chaereas to Miletus to be killed, and me to be sold into slavery."

BOOK IV

BOOK IV

THUS Callirhoe spent the night in lamentations, mourning for Chaereas who was still alive. Falling asleep for a short time, she dreamed that she saw a band of barbarian robbers applying firebrands and setting the ship on fire, while she herself brought aid to Chaereas.

Although Dionysius was very sorry to see his wife so distressed, fearing that her beauty might naturally suffer thereby, still he considered that his own love stood a better chance if she should dismiss her former husband entirely from her mind. So, wishing to demonstrate his affection and generosity, he said to her, "Get up, my dear, and make ready a tomb for that unhappy man. Why strive for what is impossible, and neglect your obvious duty? Imagine that he is standing beside you and saying, 'Bury me that I may go as soon as possible to the gates of Hades.' Even though the poor fellow's body may not be found, still, you know, it is an ancient Greek custom to provide tombs in honor even of those who are lost to sight."

He soon persuaded her, inasmuch as his advice was much to her liking. When her interest was thus engaged, her grief lessened, and rising from her couch she went to look for a spot on which to build the tomb. A place near the temple of Aphrodite attracted her, so that those living there also might have a memorial of her love. But Dionysius begrudged Chaereas this close association with Aphrodite, and wished to reserve this place for himself. Then, too, he wanted at the same time to prolong her interest, and so he said, "My dear, let us go to the city, and there before the city walls let us construct a lofty and conspicuous memorial 'that it may be seen afar by men on the deep.' Fair are the harbors of Miletus and in them the Syracusans, too, often drop anchor. Thus even among your countrymen, you shall not fail to gain credit for the honor you do him."

This proposal pleased Callirhoe, and for the time being she checked her impatience. Then, when she came to the city, she began to build on a lofty point by the shore a tomb in every way similar in shape, size, and splendor to her own in Syracuse. And this tomb, too, like that at home, was for a living person.

As soon as the work had been completed by a multitude of workers and at boundless expense, she then proceeded also to reproduce the funeral procession for

Chaereas. A special date had been announced, and on that day the population, not only of Miletus, but also of nearly all Ionia, assembled together. Two royal governors who were visitors at the time, Mithridates of Caria, and Pharnaces of Lydia, were also present. Their pretext was to do honor to Dionysius, but the truth was, they wished to see Callirhoe. The great fame of the girl was in fact known over all Asia, and the renown of Callirhoe, surpassing even that of Ariadne or Leda, was by now coming to the ears of the King of Persia.

On that occasion, however, she was found to excel even her reputation. She appeared clothed in black with flowing hair, and her gleaming face and uncovered arms made her seem more beautiful than the Homeric goddesses "of the white arms and the fair ankles." Indeed not a soul in the crowd could withstand the radiance of her beauty. Some turned their heads away as though sunlight had fallen on their eyes, others bowed low in reverence, and even the children were affected. But as for Mithridates, the governor of Caria, he fell speechless to the ground like a man unexpectedly struck by a shot from a sling, and his attendants, supporting him, could scarcely hold him up. In the procession there was carried a statue of Chaereas fashioned after his image on the seal of the ring. Yet beautiful though this image was, no one looked at it while Callirhoe was near, but she alone enthralled the eyes of all.

Who could do justice to the final scenes of this procession? When they came nearer the tomb, those who were carrying the bier set it down, and Callirhoe, walking up to it, put her arms about the image of Chaereas, and kissing it said, "You first put me in my tomb in Syracuse, and now I, in turn, do the same for you in Miletus! Our misfortunes have been as great as they are unbelievable. We have buried each other and yet neither of us has the dead body of the other. Cruel Fortune, thou hast begrudged us even in our death a common burial ground, and hast made even our dead bodies to be exiles!"

The crowd burst into lamentation and all felt pity for Chaereas, not because he was dead, but because he had been deprived of such a wife.

Thus Callirhoe was conducting a funeral for Chaereas in Miletus, while Chaereas himself was working in chains in Caria. His body was soon worn out by digging in the soil, since there was much to oppress him—weariness, neglect, chains, and more than these, his love. Though he longed for death, still some small hope that perhaps sometime he would again see Callirhoe did not permit him to die.

Then Polycharmus, his friend who had been captured with him, seeing that Chaereas was not able to work but was receiving blows and being disgracefully abused, said to their overseer, "Set aside a special place for us so that you will not count the laziness of other prisoners against us, and we will turn in our own share of the work for the day."

The overseer agreed and granted this to them. So Polycharmus, being naturally a sturdy young man and not in the toils of Love, who is a cruel tyrant, performed a double portion of the work practically by himself alone, glad to take more than his share so as to save his friend.

While these two were in all this trouble, coming at length to realize the loss of their freedom, the royal governor Mithridates returned to Caria, not at all the same man that he had been when he came to Miletus, but pale and thin from the hot and stinging wound he had received in his heart. And wasting away with love for Callirhoe, he would certainly have died if he had not met with this consolation.

Some of the workmen who were chained together with Chaereas (there were sixteen of them in all shut up in a gloomy cell) cut through their chains by night, murdered the overseer, and then attempted to run away. But they failed to make their escape because the dogs betrayed them by their barking. So when they had been hunted down, they were all imprisoned with great care in the stocks for the night, and at daylight the manager reported what had happened to his master. The latter, without even seeing them or listening to their defense, immediately ordered the sixteen men who were housed together to be crucified. Accordingly they were led out, chained together at the feet and neck, and each one carried his own cross. Thus, to the inevitable punishment, their persecutors added this external display of gruesomeness to serve as a fearful example to any other such people.

Now Chaereas remained silent as he was led off with the others, but Polycharmus while carrying his cross exclaimed, "It is on your account, Callirhoe, that we are suffering so. You are the cause of all our misfortunes!"

On hearing this speech, the manager thought there was some woman accomplice to the crime. So in order that she too might be punished and an investigation be made of the plot, he at once detached Polycharmus from the common chain, and brought him to Mithridates. The latter was reclining alone in one of the gardens, ill at ease and picturing to his mind the appearance of Callirhoe as he had seen her in her sorrow. Being completely wrapped up in his thoughts, he regarded even his servant with displeasure.

"What do you mean by disturbing me?" he said.

"I must, master," the other replied. "I have found out the chief source of that awful crime. This scoundrel here knows of some miserable woman who was an accomplice in the murder."

On hearing this, Mithridates scowled and, with a terrifying look, he said, "Tell me the name of your guilty partner in this wicked business."

But Polycharmus declared that he did not know of any; indeed, he had himself taken no part whatsoever in the deed. They called for whips; fire was brought, and preparation for torture was made.

Then one of them laid his hand on him and said, "Tell us the name of that woman who you admitted was the cause of your troubles."

"Callirhoe," said Polycharmus.

The name came as a blow to Mithridates, and he naturally imagined there was an unhappy coincidence in the names of the two women. He therefore no longer wanted to be too zealous in his investigation, or he might eventually be obliged to deal harshly with that beloved name. But when his friends and members of the household urged him on to a more careful inquiry, he said, "Have Callirhoe come here."

Accordingly they kept striking Polycharmus and asking him who she was and where they could get her. And he, poor man, though at his wit's end, still was unwilling to bring false charges against any woman and said, "There is no use making all this disturbance, trying to find someone who is not here. I meant Callirhoe of Syracuse, the daughter of the general Hermocrates."

On hearing this, Mithridates flushed deeply; he was bathed in sweat, and somehow in spite of himself a tear suddenly fell from his eyes, so that Polycharmus too became silent, and everyone there felt embarrassed. At length when he had barely recovered himself, Mithridates said, "What business have you with that Callirhoe and why did you mention her when you were on the point of death?"

"Master," he replied, "it is a long story, and it will no longer do me any good. I will not bother you with empty words at the wrong time. Besides, I am afraid that if I take too much time my friend may be gone ahead of me, and I want to die with him."

There was a general softening of hearts among his auditors; their anger changed to pity, and Mithridates was more moved than the rest.

"Do not be afraid," he said, "you will not bother me with your story. I have a kindly heart. Be brave and tell me everything. Do not omit a thing. Who are you and where did you come from? How was it that you came to Caria, and why are you wielding a shovel as a prisoner? Most of all, tell me about Callirhoe, and who your friend is."

So Polycharmus began his account. "We, the two prisoners, are Syracusans by birth. One of us is a young man who was once at the very top in Sicily, in reputation, wealth, and handsome appearance. I, on the other hand, am of small account, but I am his comrade and friend. We left our parents and sailed away from our homeland, I for his sake, and he for the sake of a girl named Callirhoe, to whom, after her seeming death, he had given a costly funeral. But grave-robbers discovered her alive and sold her to Ionia. This fact was reported to us in public assembly by the pirate Theron under torture. Then the city of Syracuse sent out a warship with delegates commissioned to recover the girl. As this ship lay at anchor by night, barbarians set it afire and slaughtered most of us, but they made prisoners of me and my friend and sold us here. For our part, we endured our misfortune patiently, but some others of our fellow prisoners, whose names we do not know, broke their chains and committed murder. Then at your command we were all

58

being led to the cross. Even at the point of death my friend would not put any blame on the girl, but I was impelled to mention her name and to call her the cause of our troubles, since it was on her account that we began our voyage."

While he was still speaking, Mithridates cried in a loud voice, "Is it Chaereas you mean?"

"Yes. My friend," said Polycharmus simply. "But I beg you, master, give orders to the executioner not to separate even the crosses on which we hang."

Tears and sighs greeted this account of his, and Mithridates sent them all after Chaereas to forestall his death. They found that the rest were already hanging on the cross and that he was just mounting upon it; and so from a distance they shouted loudly, each in his own words, "Spare him!" "Come down!" "Don't hurt him!" "Let him go!"

Accordingly the executioner put a stop to his work, and sorrowfully Chaereas descended from the cross, for he would have been glad to depart from his miserable life and his unhappy love.

As he was being escorted away, Mithridates met him and embraced him. "My dear brother," he said, "you almost betrayed me into committing a mortal sin because of your heroic but ill-advised silence."

Then he ordered his slaves at once to conduct them to the baths and to see to their physical comfort, and after their bath to clothe them with expensive Greek mantles. He himself proceeded to invite his friends to a banquet and celebrated the rescue of Chaereas. The drinking was extensive, the compliments were warm, and there was no lack of good cheer.

As the feasting progressed, Mithridates, heated with wine and passion, said, "Chaereas, it is not, I suspect, the chains and the cross for which I pity you, but rather because you have been deprived of such a wife."

"And where have you seen my Callirhoe?" cried Chaereas in astonishment.

"No longer yours," said Mithridates. "She is duly married to Dionysius of Miletus, and besides they now have a child."

On hearing this Chaereas could not restrain himself but fell at the knees of Mithridates and said, "Master, I implore you, send me back again to the cross. This is a worse torture, to compel me to live in the face of such news. Faithless Callirhoe, wickedest of all women! I have been sold in slavery for your sake; I have wielded a shovel as a slave; I have carried the cross; I have been delivered into the hands of the executioner. And you—you were living in luxury and celebrating your marriage while I was a prisoner! Was not it enough for you to become the wife of another while Chaereas was alive, but must you also become a mother?"

All now began to shed tears, and the feast took on an atmosphere of gloom. Mithridates alone was pleased at this, deriving some hope for the furtherance of his passion, since he was now in a position both to speak and act concerning Callirhoe in such a way as to seem to be aiding a friend.

"Well," he said, "It is night now, so we had better go home; but tomorrow in sober daylight let us consider this business carefully. This problem requires quite a long time to study."

Thereupon he got up and dismissed the company, and for his part went to sleep in his usual fashion, after providing special service and a room of their own for the young men.

That night brought full measure of anxiety upon them all, and no one of them could sleep. Chaereas was filled with anger, while Polycharmus tried to comfort him. Mithridates, in turn, was happy in the hope that he might, as it were, wait on the sidelines during the contest between Chaereas and Dionysius and then himself bear off Callirhoe as his prize without a struggle.

On the following day, when the discussion began, Chaereas at once demanded the right to go to Miletus and ask back his wife from Dionysius, since he was sure that Callirhoe would not remain there once she had seen him.

"So far as I am concerned," said Mithridates, "you may go. I do not want you to be parted from your wife even for a single day. I only wish that you had never left Sicily, and that misfortune had not come upon either of you. But since the whims of Fortune have involved you in this melancholy drama, you must be more prudent in your future plans. Just now your haste is due more to passion than to reason, and you are not looking ahead for what may come. Will you go alone and as a stranger to a great city, confront a man of wealth and leading position in Ionia, and expect to rob him of his wife, when she is so closely bound to him? On what resources can you rely? Hermocrates and Mithridates, your only allies, will be far away. They can feel sorry for you, but they cannot help you.

"Also, I mistrust the luck of the place. You have been already badly treated there once, but your former case is going to seem mild in comparison. You were made a prisoner to be sure, but your life was spared. You were sold as a slave, but to me as your master. Now, however, if Dionysius finds out that you are planning to corrupt his wife, what in Heaven's name can save you? You will simply deliver yourself into the hands of a cruel rival. Perhaps he will not even believe that you are Chaereas; and if he does believe you are really he, your danger will be still greater. You must be singularly ignorant of the nature of Love not to know that this god takes delight in deceit and trickery.

"I think it is best for you to try out the lady by letter first, to see whether she remembers you and wishes to leave Dionysius or if, as Homer says, all her desire is to increase the house of the man who takes her to wife. Write her a letter. Make her sad; make her happy; get her to inquire for you and call you. I will see to it that the letter is delivered. Go now and write to her."

Chaereas followed this suggestion, and when he was alone by himself, he was anxious to write, but could not because of his fast-flowing tears and trembling hand. But when this burst of self-pity was over, he began with difficulty the following letter.

Chaereas to Callirhoe: I am alive, and this is due to Mithridates, a benefactor to me and, I trust, to you as well. I was sold into Caria by barbarians who set fire to that gallant vessel, which was the flagship of your father. On it, our city had sent out an embassy to recover you. I do not know what has become of the rest of my fellow citizens, but when my friend Polycharmus and I were on the point of being killed, the mercy of our master saved us.

Yet though Mithridates has rendered me every service, he has given me such pain as to offset it all, by telling me of your marriage. Death, to be sure, I expected, since I am human, but this marriage of yours I had never looked for. Change your mind, I implore you! I cover this letter of mine with tears and kisses. I am your own Chaereas, whom once you saw when you went as a girl to Aphrodite's shrine and for whom you spent sleepless nights. Recall our marriage chamber and that mystic night when you first had experience of a husband and I of a wife. But I became jealous, you say. That is the usual thing for a lover. I have paid the penalty; I was sold, I became a slave, I was put in chains. Do not hold against me that impulsive kick I gave you. I have ascended the cross for your sake and without a word of blame for you. If you should still remember me, then my sufferings are nothing; but if you are otherwise disposed, then you have signed my death warrant.

Mithridates gave this letter to Hyginus, a very faithful servant, whom he had as the general director of all his property in Caria, and to whom he had disclosed his love. Then he, too, wrote a letter to Callirhoe, pointing out his good-will and kindly concern for her, saying that he had saved Chaereas for her sake. He counseled her not to scorn her former husband and promised that he himself would arrange matters so as to restore them to each other, if he could gain her consent as well. He sent three slaves together with Hyginus, as well as rich gifts and plenty of gold; but, to prevent suspicion, he told the other servants that he was sending these things to Dionysius. He ordered Hyginus when he arrived at Priene to leave the other servants there, and since he could speak Greek, to go on by himself in the guise of an Ionian as a spy to Miletus. Then when he had learned how to manage affairs, to bring on to Miletus those whom he had left behind in Priene.

So off he set, and was carrying out his orders, but Fortune brought about an outcome not at all in accordance with his intentions. Instead she stirred up the beginnings of still greater adventures.

When Hyginus had taken his leave for Miletus, the slaves who had been left behind in Priene, now they were deserted by their leader, started out to do some reckless spending with the pile of gold they had. In a small city filled with true Greek curiosity this extravagance on the part of strangers attracted the eyes of all to them. They were of course unknown, and by their extravagance they appeared to the citizens most likely to be robbers or, in any case, runaway slaves. Accordingly, the chief magistrate of Priene came to the inn and after a search found the gold and expensive finery. Thinking he had uncovered a robbery, he questioned the slaves as to who they were and where they got these things. In fear of torture they made known the truth, saying that Mithridates, the governor of Caria, had sent these gifts to Dionysius, and they also showed him the letters. However, the magistrate did not open them, since they were sealed on the outside, but gave them over to the public officials together with the slaves, and sent them on to Dionysius, thinking that he was doing him a good service.

Now as it happened, the latter was entertaining at dinner some of the most prominent of his fellow citizens. The banquet was a splendid one and had reached the point when the flute was playing and the melody of song was heard. In the midst of this, someone handed him this letter:

Bias, chief magistrate of Priene, to his benefactor, Dionysius—Greeting! Certain gifts and letters on their way to you from Mithridates, governor of Caria, were being plundered by worthless slaves. I arrested them and am sending them on to you.

Dionysius read this letter in the midst of the banquet and plumed himself at the thought of the royal gifts. Giving orders to cut off the seals he set about to read the letter. He saw the words: "Chaereas to Callirhoe: I am alive." Then his knees and his heart were unstrung, as Homer says, and darkness spread over his eyes. Yet, fainting though he was, he still kept his grasp on the letters for fear that another might read them. During the confusion and running about which ensued, he came to his senses, and realizing his weakness, he ordered his servants to carry him into another small chamber, because, as he said, he wanted to be quiet. Thus the banquet broke up in a melancholy way, since the guests imagined that he had suffered a stroke.

When Dionysius was by himself, he read over the letters many times and was overcome with a variety of emotions—anger, discouragement, fear, and incredulity. He did not at all believe that Chaereas was alive, because that was not what he wanted. Rather he suspected an adulterous plot on the part of Mithridates who, by raising expectations of Chaereas, was hoping to corrupt the mind of Callirhoe.

Therefore, when day came, he kept a more careful watch over his wife to prevent anyone from approaching her or telling her anything of the news from Caria. Meantime he himself devised the following means of protection.

Quite opportunely Pharnaces, the governor of Lydia and Ionia, was visiting them, a man who was considered to be really the greatest of those officials sent by the king to rule the maritime provinces. Dionysius approached him—they were friends, you see—and demanded a private interview.

"Sir," he said, "I beg you, help me and yourself at the same time. That archvillain Mithridates, who is jealous of you too, enjoyed my hospitality and now he is trying to break up my marriage, and has sent scandalous letters and money to my wife."

At this point he read the letters aloud and explained the scheme. Pharnaces was glad to hear this story, partly, to be sure, on account of Mithridates, since they had had not a few disagreeable contacts as neighbors, but still more so because of his own infatuation. You see, he too was ardently in love with Callirhoe, and it was for her sake that he made his frequent visits to Miletus, inviting Dionysius to banquets together with his wife. So he promised he would help him in every way he could; and he secretly wrote this letter.

Pharnaces, governor of Lydia and Ionia, to his own master Artaxerxes, King of Kings—Greeting! Dionysius of Miletus is your hereditary slave, faithful and zealous toward your house. He has complained to me that Mithridates, governor of Caria, after being his guest, is now trying to corrupt his wife. This is bringing not only serious discredit, but actual confusion, upon your government. Every illegal act of a governor is open to blame, and especially this one, for Dionysius is the most powerful of the Ionians, and the beauty of his wife is widely known, so that the scandal cannot escape notice.

When this letter was brought to him, the Great King read it to his friends and considered what he must do. Many diverse opinions were expressed. Those that were jealous of Mithridates or were bidding for the governorship thought that a plot against the wife of so prominent a man should not be overlooked. On the other hand, those who were more easygoing or who felt respect for Mithridates—and he had many such distinguished friends—were not content that a man of his note should be snatched to ruin at the hint of scandal. Since the opinions were evenly balanced, the king made no decision on that day, but postponed the investigation.

When night came, he was overcome with indignation at this wrong, feeling that it concerned the proprieties of kingship, and yet he felt some caution regarding the future, since Mithridates had an opportunity to defy him. And so he set out to summon him to trial. Then another feeling advised him to send for the beautiful wife as well. The fact was that the influence of wine and darkness on his loneliness had recalled to the king's mind that portion of the letter, too, and also the report that a certain Callirhoe was the most beautiful woman in Ionia urged him on in his purpose. This indeed was the one point in which the king blamed Pharnaces, namely, that he had failed to add the name of the wife in his letter. However, in the doubtful hope that perhaps, though not the same, she might prove even superior to the one people were talking of, he decided to summon the wife as well.

And so he wrote to Pharnaces, "Send Dionysius of Miletus, my slave, and send his wife with him;" and to Mithridates, "Come here to make your defense against the charge of plotting to corrupt Dionysius' wife."

Mithridates was greatly shocked and quite at a loss concerning the cause of this slanderous accusation, when Hyginus returned and reported what had happened about the servants. And so, betrayed as he was by the letters, he resolved not to go to Babylon, dreading the disgrace of the charges, and the anger of the king, but decided rather to capture Miletus and to kill Dionysius, the cause of his troubles, and then to seize Callirhoe and revolt from the king.

"Why be in a hurry to surrender your liberty to the hands of a master?" he said to himself. "Perhaps you can be the winner by staying right here. The king is a long way off, and his officers are of little account; and even if he should wipe you out in some other way, you can be no worse off. But in any case do not desert those two greatest of blessings, love and power. Supremacy is a glorious memorial and with Callirhoe death is sweet!"

While he was still considering these matters and making his preparations for revolt, a messenger came saying that Dionysius had now set out from Miletus and was bringing Callirhoe with him. This news brought more grief to Mithridates than the summons which called him to trial, and so in tearful protest against his lot he said, "What hope is there now if I do stay? Luck is against me in every possible way. Well, perhaps the king may have pity on me since I have done no wrong; but even if I should have to die, I am going to see Callirhoe once more. At the trial I shall keep Chaereas and Polycharmus with me, not only for moral support, but as witnesses, too."

Accordingly he commanded all his retinue to accompany him, and set out from Caria with a stout heart, for surely, he thought, he would not be accounted guilty. So they saw him off, not with tears but with sacrificial rites and a solemn procession.

Now while the god of love was sending out this one expedition from Caria, he was dispatching another from Ionia which was even more notable, since it had the still more striking and regal appeal of beauty. Indeed, the fame of the girl ran on before her, reporting to all men the coming of Callirhoe, known far and wide as the masterpiece of Nature, "like unto Artemis or golden Aphrodite." The story of the coming trial made her still more conspicuous. Whole cities came out to meet her. The streets were crowded with those that ran to see her; and to all the girl seemed even to surpass the report made of her.

The congratulations which Dionysius received caused him pain, and the very magnitude of his good fortune made him all the more timid, for, educated as he was, he knew well in his heart that Love is ever fickle. That is why poets and sculptors associate him with the bow and the torch, things that are most light and unstable. He recalled to mind ancient stories of the many transfigurations of beautiful women; in fact, everything frightened Dionysius. He looked on all men as his rivals, not merely his future opponent in court, but the very judge, so that he was sorry that he had been so hasty in telling this affair to Pharnaces, when he "could have slept and had his beloved with him." It was, in fact, one thing to keep watch over Callirhoe in Miletus, and quite another in the midst of all Asia.

However, he concealed his secret to the end and did not confide to his wife the reason for their going, but his pretext was that the king was sending for him, because he wished to consult with him about affairs in Ionia. Callirhoe was troubled at being brought so far from the sea of the Greeks, for as long as she could see the harbors of Miletus it seemed to her that Syracuse was near. Then too she used to get great comfort from the presence of Chaereas' tomb there.

BOOK V

BOOK V

How Callirhoe, the most beautiful of women, was married to Chaereas, the handsomest of men, through the skillful management of Aphrodite; and how, when Chaereas had struck her in a jealous rage, she had apparently died and then, after being given a costly funeral, was restored to consciousness in the tomb; how next grave-robbers carried her off by night from Sicily, and, sailing to Ionia, sold her to Dionysius; then, the love of Dionysius and the fidelity of Callirhoe toward Chaereas; the wedding that was forced by the imminence of her confinement; the confession of Theron and the voyage of Chaereas in search of his wife; his capture and subsequent sale to Caria with his friend Polycharmus; how Mithridates came to recognize Chaereas on the point of death, and exerted himself to restore the lovers to each other; how Dionysius, discovering this from the letters, accused him to Pharnaces, and he to the king; and how the king summoned them both to judgment—all this has been explained in our previous account. I shall now relate what followed.

Until they reached Syria and Cilicia, Callirhoe bore her exile lightly, for she could still hear Greek spoken and could see the ocean which led back to Syracuse. But when she arrived at the Euphrates River, the gateway to the extensive land of the Great King, beyond which the great mainland begins, then she fell prey to homesickness, longing for her family and despairing of ever returning again. So standing at the river bank and telling them all to draw back except Plangon, her one loyal friend, she began to speak as follows:

"Cruel Fortune, who dost delight in persecuting one lone girl, thou didst shut me living in the tomb, and didst bring me forth not out of pity, but to deliver me to pirates. Theron and the sea combined to effect my exile, and I, the daughter of Hermocrates, have been sold into slavery! Furthermore—a thing even harder to bear than my friendless state—I inspired a man's love and so became the wife of another, while Chaereas was still alive.

"But thou dost now begrudge me even this, for thou dost no longer banish me to Ionia. There the land which thou didst give me, though foreign, was still Greek, and there I had a great consolation—'I sit by the sea.' But now thou dost cast me forth from familiar surroundings and I am parted from my homeland by a whole world. Thou hast once more robbed me of Miletus, as before of Syracuse. I am

69

being taken away beyond the Euphrates and I, born on an island, am shut within the clefts of a barbarian land where there is no more sea. What ship sailing from Sicily can I now expect? I am being torn away even from your tomb, Chaereas. Who is to pour libations for you, dear heart? Hereafter Bactra and Susa shall be my home and my tomb. I shall cross thy stream but once, Euphrates! Indeed, I fear not so much the length of the journey, but rather that there too someone may think me beautiful."

With these words she kissed the ground, and then stepping on board the ferry, she crossed to the other side.

Now Dionysius had an elaborate retinue of his own, since he wanted to impress his wife with the great wealth at his command. However, their progress was rendered still more regal by the kindly attentions of the natives of the country. One nation would escort them on to the next, and each governor would turn them over to the care of his neighbor; such was the enthralling power of beauty over them all. Also, still another hope warmed the hearts of these barbarians—namely, that this woman would gain great power; and for that reason each was eager to offer her hospitality or in some way or other to lay up for himself future favor with her.

Such then was their situation. Mithridates, in turn, was making his way through Armenia in great haste, much afraid that the very fact that he was following in the footsteps of Callirhoe might be held against him by the king, and at the same time being eager to get there first and to consolidate his preparations for the trial. Accordingly, when he had arrived at Babylon—for that was where the king was staying—he rested during that day in his own quarters, since all the governors have lodgings assigned to them there, but on the following day he arrived at the palace gates and greeted his colleagues among the Persians. Then after first conferring gifts upon Artaxates, the eunuch, who was a highly important and powerful person in the service of the king, he said, "Announce my presence to the king and say, 'Your slave, Mithridates, is here to acquit himself of a slanderous charge made by a Greek, and to pay his deep respects.' "

Not long afterward the eunuch came out and replied, "It is the king's wish not to do Mithridates any injustice, but you shall stand trial when Dionysius, too, arrives."

With a deep bow Mithridates took his leave, and when he was by himself, he called Chaereas and said to him, "I have been playing with fire. I volunteered to restore Callirhoe to you, and now they charge me with a crime. That letter of yours, which you wrote to your wife, Dionysius says was written by me, and he assumes that he has proof of adultery, since he is convinced that you are dead. Let him remain so convinced until the trial. Then you can make a sudden appearance. This is the one return for my kindness to you which I claim. Keep yourself in hiding; steel yourself not to see Callirhoe nor to make any inquiries about her."

70

Chaereas consented, though sore against his will, and tried to hide his feelings, but the tears ran down his cheeks. However, he said, "Master, I shall do as you order," and went off to the room in which he was lodging with his friend, Polycharmus. There, throwing himself to the floor and tearing his garments, "with both hands he took the dark dust and poured it over his head and defiled his comely face."

Then, with a sob, he said, "Callirhoe, we are so close, and yet we cannot see each other! But you are not to blame at all, because you do not know that your Chaereas is still alive. Rather, I am the most disloyal man on earth ever to have accepted a command not to see you. Coward that I am—to cling to life and submit to such tyranny! If someone had told you to do this, you would have refused to live."

While Polycharmus was trying to comfort him, Dionysius, too, had come near to Babylon. Rumor ran ahead to occupy the city, proclaiming to all the coming of a woman of superhuman and heavenly beauty, the like of whom the sun does not see on earth. Now, barbarian natures are insanely romantic, and so every house and every lane was filled with her fame. The report about her reached even the king himself, so that he too asked the eunuch, Artaxates, whether the Milesian woman had yet arrived.

This publicity surrounding his wife had long since caused pain to Dionysius, for it meant insecurity; but when he was about to enter Babylon, he then became still more distressed. Groaning aloud, he said to himself, "This is no longer Miletus, your home, Dionysius, though there, too, you had to guard against schemers. A risky and short-sighted business, this, to bring Callirhoe to Babylon, where there are so many men like Mithridates! Menelaus could not keep Helen safe in strait-laced Sparta, but a barbarian shepherd boy outwitted him, king though he was. There are many men like Paris among the Persians. Can you not see the dangers and the portents? Whole cities come out to meet us and governors offer us hospitality. Matters have already become ominous enough, and the king has not yet seen her. The only hope of safety lies in smuggling her through. If she can remain hidden, she will be kept safe."

With these reflections, he mounted his horse, but left Callirhoe in the carriage and tightly closed the awning. Perhaps it would have turned out as he wished, had not the following incident occurred.

The wives of some of the most prominent Persians appeared before Statira, the queen, and one of them said to her, "Your Majesty, a worthless Greek woman is coming to jeopardize our own fair ladies, whom all men from of old have admired for their beauty, and now in our times the glory of Persian womanhood is in danger of being destroyed. So we had better consider how to prevent our humiliation at the hands of this stranger."

The queen, who disbelieved the report, laughed and said, "The Greeks are beggarly braggarts, and that is why they show such great admiration for such small matters. They speak of the 'beauty' of Callirhoe in the same breath with the 'wealth' of Dionysius. So when she comes, let some one of us appear beside her and cast this poor slave in the shade."

All the women bowed low to the queen and expressed their admiration of her plan, and at first as with one accord they cried, "Your Majesty, if only you could be seen yourself!"

After that their opinions were much scattered and they proceeded to name the women who were most noted for their beauty. A formal election followed as in the theater, and their first choice was Rhodogyne, the daughter of Zopyrus and the wife of Megabyzus, a great beauty and very famous. What Callirhoe was to Ionia, Rhodogyne was to Asia. The women took her and dressed her, each one contributing something of her own to her adornment. The queen, too, gave her bracelets and a necklace.

Thus, when they had well prepared her for the contest, she made her appearance as though formally to receive Callirhoe. In fact, she had an appropriate excuse, in that she was the sister of Pharnaces, who had written the letter to the king about Dionysius. All Babylon poured out to view the sight and the crowd blocked the gates. In the most conspicuous position Rhodogyne waited with her royal escort. She stood there, delicate and high-bred, as though awaiting the challenge, and all looked at her and murmured to each other, "We have won! The Persian lady will eclipse the stranger. Let her stand the comparison if she can Then the Greeks will realize that they boast too much."

Meantime Dionysius had arrived, and when he was informed that the kinswoman of Pharnaces was there, he jumped down from his horse and approached her with words of friendly greeting. But she blushed and said, "I wish to welcome my sister," and at the same time she came up to the carriage.

And so it was no longer possible for Callirhoe to remain concealed, and Dionysius, much against his will and sighing deeply with embarrassment, asked her to come out. At that moment all the crowd strained not only their eyes but, so to speak, their very souls, and nearly fell over each other, in their eagerness to see her, each before his neighbor, and to get as near as possible.

Callirhoe's face gleamed with a radiance which held the eyes of all, just as when a great light is suddenly seen on a dark night. Overcome with astonishment, the Persians bowed reverently, and no one appeared to notice the presence of Rhodogyne. The latter, also, recognized her defeat, and being unable to retire and not desiring to attract attention, she entered under the awning with Callirhoe, surrendering herself to her as the victor.

Thus the wagon advanced, closed to view, and the people, no longer able to see Callirhoe, sought to kiss the vehicle itself.

When the king heard of the arrival of Dionysius, he told the eunuch Artaxates to carry a message to him, saying, "Since you are bringing a charge against a man trusted with high office, you should not have been so slow. But I forgive you your negligence since you were traveling with a woman. Just now however, I am celebrating a holy day, and am busy with the sacrifices. Thirty days from now I will listen to the trial."

Dionysius bowed low and retired.

From then on preparations for the trial were made by both sides as though for a most important battle. The Persian public was divided, and all those of the governors' faction sided with Mithridates. He was, you see, from Bactra in the north and had later changed his residence to Caria. Dionysius, on the other hand, held the favor of the common people, since they considered that he had been unlawfully wronged by this plot against his wife, who—and this was the main point—was of such beauty. Indeed, not even the women's quarters among the Persians remained unaffected, but there, too, different sides were taken. Those of them who prided themselves on their beauty were jealous of Callirhoe and wanted her to be disgraced as a result of the trial. But the majority, who were envious of their local rivals, joined their prayers for the popular success of the stranger.

Of the principals each felt that he had victory in his very hands; Dionysius, since he trusted to the letter which Mithridates sent to Callirhoe in the name of Chaereas (for of course he never expected that Chaereas was alive); Mithridates, on the other hand, since he was able to produce Chaereas, was confident that defeat was impossible. However, he pretended to be afraid and called in advocates, so as to render his defense still more brilliant by its unexpected character.

During these thirty days both men and women among the Persians had no other topic of conversation than this trial, so that if the truth must be told, all Babylon became a courthouse. All considered the delay excessive, the king himself no less than the others. What Olympic games or Eleusinian nightly celebrations ever held the prospect of such enthusiasm?

When the official day finally arrived, the king took his seat. There is a special room of extraordinary size and beauty in the palace set apart for a courtroom; in its midst is placed a throne for the king, and on either side others for his friends who, because of their rank and ability, belong to the high command. Round about the throne there stand captains and division commanders and the most distinguished of the freedmen of the king, so that of that august tribunal one might well say with Homer, "Now the gods sat by Zeus and held assembly." Those subject to their judgment are brought forward in silence and trepidation.

Now on this occasion Mithridates appeared first, early in the morning, escorted by friends and relatives. He was by no means bright and cheerful but rather pitiable instead, as befits an accused man. Dionysius followed after him, dressed in Greek fashion with a Milesian mantle and holding the letters in his hand. When they were ushered in, they bowed low. Then the king ordered the clerk to read the letters, both that of Pharnaces and the one which he himself had written in answer, so that his fellow judges might know how the suit had been instituted. Following the reading of the letters, there came a burst of commendation from the audience who marveled at the moderation and justice of the king. Then after silence had been restored, Dionysius, as plaintiff, was required to speak first.

All were gazing at him, when Mithridates said, "Sire, I do not wish to anticipate my defense, but I know the proper procedure. Before the speeches begin, all who are essential to the trial must be present. Where, then, is the woman about whom you are to judge? You decided, as shown by your letter, that she was indispensable, and you wrote for her to be present, and she is here. Do not allow Dionysius to hide away the principal object and reason for this whole affair."

To this Dionysius replied, "This is a scandalous thing, to bring another man's wife before the public contrary to his wishes, when she is neither the plaintiff nor the defendant. Now if she had actually been wronged, then she would necessarily be present for examination, but as it is, you laid your schemes against her without her knowledge, and I do not need the lady as either principal or supporting witness. Why, then, must she be here, since she has no actual part in the trial?"

These words of Dionysius were technically true, but they carried no conviction, since everyone was eager to see Callirhoe. Thus, in view of the King's embarrassment at demanding her presence, his friends held out the letter as a pretext, for she really had been summoned as a necessary witness.

"How absurd it is," people remarked, "for her to have come all the way from Ionia and then to default, now she is in Babylon."

Now that the presence of Callirhoe, too, was thus determined upon, Dionysius, who previously had told her nothing, but had consistently concealed the reason for their journey to Babylon, was afraid to bring her into court so suddenly and unawares, since it was very likely that she would become extremely angry at the deceit. Consequently he had the case postponed until the following day.

Thus for the time the court was dismissed. On arriving at his house, Dionysius, like the wise and experienced man that he was, offered such arguments to the girl as might be most persuasive under the circumstances, touching lightly and tactfully on each point. Nevertheless Callirhoe could not of course refrain from tears as she listened, and when Chaereas' name was mentioned, she burst into sobs, and was greatly distressed at the prospect of the trial.

"This is the one thing," she said, "which was yet lacking in my misfortunes— to be dragged into court! I have died and have been buried, I have been the victim of tomb-robbers, I have been sold, I have been a slave, and now, here I am, a prisoner at the bar! Was it not enough for thee, O Fortune, to have unjustly accused me to Chaereas? Hast thou also given Dionysius grounds for suspecting me of unfaithfulness? At that time thou didst parade my disgrace to the tomb; now it is to the court of the king. I have become a by-word to Asia and to Europe. How can I bear to face the judge? What dreadful things must I hear? O treacherous beauty, given me by nature only to be overwhelmed with scandal! The daughter of Hermocrates is being brought to trial and she does not have her father to defend her! When others enter the courtroom they beg for kindness and favor, but as for me, I fear that I may please the eye of the judge."

With such lamentations as these she spent the whole day in discouragement, and Dionysius was more disheartened than she.

When night came, she saw herself in a dream, once more a girl in Syracuse, entering the sacred precinct of Aphrodite and returning from it; now she was looking at Chaereas and observing her wedding day; the whole city was decked with garlands and she herself was being escorted by her father and mother to the home of the groom. Just as she was about to kiss Chaereas, she started up from sleep and called Plangon. Dionysius, you see, had already gotten up to rehearse his speech for the trial.

She told her about the dream, and Plangon replied, "Cheer up, mistress! You ought to be happy! That is a good dream that you have had. You are going to be rid of all your worries. Things are really going to be just as they seemed to you in the dream. Go to the king's court as though to the temple of Aphrodite. Remember what you were and get back that beauty you had as a bride."

With these words, she dressed Callirhoe and adorned her, and in spite of herself Callirhoe felt cheered in heart at this apparent prophecy of the future.

So, early in the morning, a milling crowd gathered about the palace, and the streets were full to the edge of the city. All were hurrying together, ostensibly to listen to the trial, but really to see Callirhoe, who, just as she had formerly surpassed the beauty of other women, so now appeared to surpass herself. Accordingly when she entered the courtroom she looked just as the divine poet says that Helen did, when she appeared to "them that were with Priam and Panthöos and Thymoëtes, . . . being elders of the people." At the sight of her, admiring silence fell, "and each one uttered a prayer that he might be her bedfellow." Indeed, if Mithridates had been compelled to speak first, he would have had no voice, for he had received, as it were, on the unhealed wound of his heart still another blow more violent than that of his former passion. But Dionysius began the debate as follows:

"Your Majesty, I thank you for the honor which you have shown to me as well as to the cause of morality and the institution of marriage. You have not allowed a private citizen to be a victim of the schemes of a high official, but you have summoned him here, so that by visiting punishment upon his insolence and wantonness toward me you may put an end to such things in other cases. The crime deserves a still greater punishment because of the man who committed it. For it was

Mithridates, not an enemy, but my guest and my friend, who violated my confidence, looking moreover not to any of my material possessions but rather to that which is dearer to me than body and soul, my wife. Yet it was his duty, if any one else had thus offended me, to come to my aid himself, if not out of friendship to me, at least out of respect for you, his king. You have intrusted him with a position of highest importance, and he has proved himself unfit and has brought shame upon it; even more than that, he has betrayed you who trusted him with that office.

"I, too, am not unaware that the appeals of Mithridates, as well as the power and means at his disposal in this contest, are not on the same low level as ours, but, Your Majesty, I have confidence in your justice and in the sanctity of marriage and in the laws which you uphold with equality to all. If you do intend to acquit him, it would be much better not to have summoned him at all. At that time, you see, everyone was in fear, believing that crime once brought to justice was sure to be punished. But if after judgment before you a man fails of punishment, thereafter he will feel nothing but contempt.

"My story is clear and brief. I am the husband of Callirhoe, and by her I have now been made a father. I married her, not as a maid, but as the widow of a former husband, Chaereas by name, who is now long dead and whose tomb stands near our home. When Mithridates came to Miletus and was presented to my wife, as the laws of hospitality demand, he then proceeded to act not as a friend nor as a man of self-restraint and decency, such as you wish those to be whom you intrust with state government, but showed himself lewd and overbearing. Understanding well the modesty and the loyal affection of my wife, he realized it was impossible to win her over by arguments or bribes, so he invented a trick for her seduction which, as he thought, would be most persuasive. He pretended that her former husband, Chaereas, was still alive and forged letters in his name which he sent to Callirhoe by means of his slaves. But, O Fortune, thy jealous ill-will appointed a king worthy of the name, and the providence of the other gods made these letters to be discovered. Bias, the chief magistrate of Priene, dispatched these slaves together with the letters to me, and I, detecting the fraud, reported them to Pharnaces, governor of Lydia and Ionia, and he to you.

"I have now given you the story of the case which you are judging. The conclusions are unescapable. One of two things must follow, either that Chaereas is still alive, or else Mithridates stands convicted of seduction. He cannot even make claim that he was ignorant of the death of Chaereas, because while he was there in Miletus we erected the memorial to him and he joined in our mourning. However, when Mithridates wishes to commit adultery, he can raise the dead! I conclude by reading the letter which he sent from Caria to Miletus by the hands of his own servants. Take the letter and read; 'I, Chaereas, am alive.' Let Mithridates make that good and gain his acquittal. But just think, Your Majesty, how unabashed an adulterer is, when he utters lies even against a dead man!"

With these words Dionysius aroused the emotions of his audience and he un-questionably had their vote. The king, too, moved to anger, looked toward Mithridates with a bitter and gloomy expression.

Not at all disconcerted, the latter said, "Your Majesty, you are a just and kindly man; so do not condemn me until you hear both sides of the story. Do not allow a mere Greek, who has cleverly put together some false slander against me, to gain greater credit with you than the actual truth. I am aware that the beauty of this woman weighs suspiciously against me, for it seems entirely credible for any man to wish to seduce Callirhoe. But as for myself, I have lived all my life until now without reproach, and this is the first scandal to which I have been subjected. But even if I actually were a dissolute and lewd person, still the fact that I have been intrusted by you with the welfare of these great states would have made me a better man. Who is so senseless as to prefer to lose such blessings as these for the sake of a moment's pleasure, infamous in itself? Furthermore, if I had had a guilty conscience, I could even have taken an exception to the indictment, inasmuch as Dionysius is not bringing suit in behalf of a wife legally married to him. Rather, he bought her when she was offered for sale, and the law which deals with adultery does not apply to slaves. Let him first read to you the document of emancipation and then let him talk of marriage.

"Do you dare to call her your wife whom the pirate Theron sold to you for a thousand pieces of silver when, too, he had snatched her from a tomb? 'But,' he says, 'she was free when I bought her.' Then you are a kidnaper and not a husband.

"However, I shall now make my defense as though to her husband. You may call that purchase a marriage, and the purchase price her dowry. For today, the Syracusan woman may appear as a Milesian. Now, Sire, hear how even so I have done no wrong to Dionysius either as her husband or her master.

"In the first place, he charges me with adultery, not committed, but, as he says, intended, and being unable to state the fact, he reads us pointless letters. Yet the laws exact punishment only for actual deeds.

"You bring us a letter. I might say, 'I did not write it. That is not my hand-writing. It is Chaereas who is looking for Callirhoe; try him therefore for adultery.'

" 'Yes,' he says, 'but Chaereas is dead, and you solicited my wife in the name of a dead man.'

"Dionysius, this provocation you offer me is one which will do you no good whatsoever. I call you to witness, I am your friend and ally. Retract this charge. It is for your own good. Beg the king to dismiss the suit. Recant, and say, 'Mithridates has done no wrong. I blamed him without reason.' But if you persist, you will be sorry. You will cast the vote against yourself. I warn you, you will lose Callirhoe. The king will find not me, but you, the adulterer!"

With these words he fell silent. All glanced at Dionysius, wishing to learn whether in the face of this alternative he would retract his charge or would persist in it firmly; for what this riddle of Mithridates meant, they did not understand, but they conceived that Dionysius knew. Yet he, too, was in ignorance, since he never could have suspected that Chaereas was still alive. And so he spoke.

"Say whatever you want," he said, "you shall not deceive me with your sophistries and specious threats. Dionysius shall never be found to have falsified his accusation."

Interrupting him at this point, Mithridates raised his voice and exclaimed as though at a séance, "Dread powers who rule Heaven and Hell, come to the aid of a virtuous man! Often have I duly prayed and made rich sacrifices to you. Return to me, then, the reward for my piety, now I am falsely accused. Grant to me Chaereas, at least for this trial. Appear, noble spirit! Thy Callirhoe is calling thee! Take thy stand between the two of us, Dionysius and myself, and tell the king which of us is the adulterer."

While he was still speaking—for so it had been arranged—Chaereas himself stepped forward. Callirhoe, on seeing him, cried aloud, "Chaereas, are you really alive?" and she started to rush toward him. But Dionysius checked her and, standing between them, would not permit them to embrace each other.

Who could worthily tell of the appearance of the courtroom then? What dramatist ever produced so incredible a situation on the stage? Indeed, you might have thought that you were in a theater, filled with a multitude of conflicting passions. All alike were there—tears, joy, astonishment, pity, disbelief, prayer. They blessed Chaereas and rejoiced with Mithridates; they grieved with Dionysius; they were in doubt what to do about Callirhoe. She herself was most confused of all and stood there speechless, gazing with wide-opened eyes toward Chaereas alone, and I think on that occasion even the king himself may well have wished that he were Chaereas.

However, warfare among all rivals is common and easy enough, and for these two the very sight of the prize stirred up their mutual enmity all the more, so that if it had not been for their reverence for the king, they would have even rushed to blows with each other. As it was, their quarrel was confined to words.

"I am her first husband," said Chaereas.

"But I am more faithful," replied Dionysius.

"Did I ever divorce my wife?"

"No, but you put her in the tomb."

"Show me the decree of divorce."

"You can see the tomb, I suppose?"

"Her father gave her to me."

"Yes, but she gave herself to me."

"You are unworthy of the daughter of Hermocrates."

"And you who have been Mithridates' slave are more so?"

"I demand Callirhoe back."

"And I am keeping her."

"You are holding another man's wife."

"You killed your own."

"Adulterer!"

"Murderer!"

Such was their exchange of thrust and parry, and the others all listened with no small pleasure. Callirhoe meanwhile stood weeping with eyes toward the ground, loving Chaereas, yet ashamed for Dionysius' sake.

The king, dismissing all the rest, counseled with his friends, no longer on the case of Mithridates, for he had made a brilliant defense, but whether he ought to render his decision on the disposal of the girl. Some of them thought that such a judgment was not proper for the king. "It was quite natural," they said, "for you to listen to the charges against Mithridates, because he was a royal governor;" but these now were all private citizens. The majority, however, gave the opposite advice, because the girl's father had been of considerable aid to the royal house, and because the king was not calling in this case before him from outside, but it was practically a part of the one which he was already judging. The most honest reason, however, they refused to admit: namely, that Callirhoe's beauty was hard to banish from their sight.

Accordingly he recalled those whom he had dismissed and said, "I grant acquittal to Mithridates and tomorrow he shall receive gifts from me and go back to his own governorship. But now let Chaereas and Dionysius plead their cases according to their respective claims to this woman, since it is my duty to watch out for the interests of the daughter of Hermocrates, who vanquished the Athenians who are most hateful to me and to the Persians."

And so when the words of acquittal had been spoken, Mithridates bowed low. The others, however, were filled with consternation, and the king, seeing their difficulties, said, "I will not hurry you, but I will allow you to come for the trial fully prepared. I grant you a postponement of five days. Meantime my queen, Statira, will take care of Callirhoe, since it is not right that she should appear for judgment in the company of either husband, when she is to stand trial on that very matter."

Thus all the rest went out from the courtroom in a gloomy frame of mind, and Mithridates alone was happy. He received his gifts and, after waiting one night, set out at early dawn for Caria, more resplendent than before.

The king's eunuchs took Callirhoe and brought her to the queen without warning her beforehand, for when the king sends, there is no announcement. When Statira suddenly caught sight of her, she started up from her couch, thinking that it was Aphrodite who stood before her; for, you see, she held that goddess in especial honor. Callirhoe in turn bowed low, and the eunuch, perceiving her agitation, said, "This is Callirhoe. The king has sent her for you to care for until the trial begins."

Statira was delighted to hear this, and in view of this honor, she dismissed all feminine antagonism and became very kindly disposed toward Callirhoe. In fact, she was delighted with this mark of confidence.

So taking her by the hand, she said, "Take courage, my girl, and stop your weeping. The king is kind. You shall have the husband you wish, and after the trial your marriage shall be celebrated with still greater renown. Go now and rest. I can see you are worn out and your heart is still much disturbed."

These words sounded sweet to Callirhoe, who was indeed longing for quiet. Then, when she lay on her couch, and they had left her to rest, she put her hands to her eyes and said, "Have you really seen Chaereas? Was that my Chaereas, or am I deceived in this, too? Perhaps Mithridates conjured up a ghost to support his case. They say there are magicians among the Persians. And yet he could speak and told them everything as though he knew. Then, how could he bear it, not to put his arms about me? We were separated without even having kissed each other."

In the midst of these thoughts, she heard the sound of footsteps and the loud voices of women. They were all hurrying to the queen, thinking they had a splendid chance to see Callirhoe. But Statira said, "We must let her alone. She is not feeling well. We still have four days to see her, listen to her, and speak with her."

Regretfully they went away and came again early the next day. This was repeated every day with great eagerness, so that the palace became quite thronged with people. Moreover, the king, too, went in to see the women more frequently, as though to visit Statira. Rich gifts were sent to Callirhoe, but she refused to accept them from anyone, and maintained her appearance of a girl in distress, and sat there dressed in black and without adornments. This rendered her beauty still more brilliant. But when the queen asked her which husband she preferred she made no answer but only wept.

While Callirhoe was thus situated, Dionysius, relying on his steadfast nature and disciplined habits, tried hard to bear nobly what had befallen him. Yet the incredible nature of this mischance might easily have driven even a stalwart man to madness. His passion burned more hotly even than in Miletus; for while at the beginning he had been in love only with her beauty, now many things increased the flame—their intimacy and the benefit of children, as well as her ingratitude and his jealousy, and above all the unexpectedness of it all.

At any rate, thus inflamed he kept shouting many times, "What sort of Protesilaus is this who has risen from the dead to vex me? What power of Hell have I thus offended to discover a rival in a dead man whose tomb is on my property? Lady Aphrodite, thou hast played me false; yet for thee I set up a temple on my estate and to thee I make many sacrifices! Why didst thou show Callirhoe to me, when thou wert not to keep her for me? Why didst thou make me a father when I am not even a husband?"

Meantime he took his son in his arms, and weeping he said, "Poor child, whose birth I once thought meant happiness to me! Now rather it is a burden. In you I have the heritage of your mother and a token of my unhappy love. Though you are a child, still you are not wholly unaware of the misfortunes of your father. It is a sorry journey on which we have come. We should never have left Miletus. Babylon has brought our ruin. I met defeat in the first trial when Mithridates spoke against me, and I dread the second encounter still more. The danger may not be greater, but the ominous prelude to the case has left me with scarcely a hope. I have been deprived of my wife without a hearing, and though she is mine, I am contending for her with another man. What is still worse, I do not know which of us Callirhoe prefers.

"But you, my child, can learn this from her as your mother. So go right now and beseech her for your father's sake. Weep and kiss her and say, 'Mother, my father loves you,' but offer no reproaches.

"What is that you say, servant? They will not permit us to enter the palace? What dreadful tyranny! They shut the door upon a son who comes to plead his father's cause to his mother!"

While Dionysius spent his time until the trial balancing the issue between passion and reason, Chaereas was overcome with a grief that could not be comforted. Pretending to be indisposed, he told Polycharmus to escort Mithridates on his way, as the benefactor of them both. Then, when he was left alone, he fastened a noose and as he was about to step up to use it, he said, "I would die more happy, if I were ascending the cross which a false accusation set up for me when I was a slave in Caria. Then I was taking my leave of life in the false belief that Callirhoe loved me, but now I have lost not only my life but even the consolation of death. Callirhoe saw me and did not come to me. She did not kiss me. Though I stood by her side, she felt shame before another man. She need not be embarrassed! I shall anticipate the decision. I shall not wait for an inglorious end. I know that I am a weak opponent to Dionysius, alien and poor as I am, and an outsider now. God bless you, my wife, for wife I shall call you, even though you may love another! I am going away and will not cause you trouble in your marriage. Be rich! Live in luxury! Enjoy the lavishness of Ionia! Hold to the man you want!

"But one last favor, Callirhoe, I beg of you, when your Chaereas now is truly dead. When I am gone, visit my corpse and, if you can, weep over it. This will be greater in my sight than immortality. And as you bend over my tombstone, say, 'I see the legend, "Both husband and child." Chaereas, now truly you are gone. Now you are dead, and I was about to choose you before the king's tribunal.' I shall hear you, my wife. Perhaps, too, I will believe you. You will make me more respected to the gods below. 'If even in the house of Hades the dead forget their dead, yet will I even there be mindful of thy dear self.' "

With such lamentations as these he kissed the noose and said, "You are my comfort and support. Through you I am the victor. You show me greater love than Callirhoe."

When he was stepping up and fixing the noose about his neck, his friend, Polycharmus, came upon him and restrained him by force like the madman he was, since he could no longer comfort him with words.

Meantime the day fixed for the trial came around.

BOOK VI

BOOK VI

Wᴴᴇɴ, on the following day, the king was about to render his decision whether Callirhoe should be the wife of Chaereas or of Dionysius, all Babylon was in suspense, and people both at home and meeting in the streets said to each other, "Tomorrow is Callirhoe's wedding. Which of the two will be the lucky man?"

The city was divided, and the supporters of Chaereas argued, "He was her first husband; he married her as a girl; and it was a love match. Her father gave her to him; her fatherland put her in the tomb. He did not desert his bride; he was not deserted by her. Dionysius did not win her consent; he did not really marry her. Pirates put her up for sale; but it is not possible to buy a free-born woman."

The supporters of Dionysius, on the other hand, replied in turn, "He got her away from a pirate band when she was about to be killed; he paid a thousand pieces of silver to rescue her. First he rescued her, then he married her; but Chaereas married her and then caused her death. Callirhoe ought to remember this marriage. The fact that they have a child in common is well known and favors the victory of Dionysius."

Such were the arguments of the men. But the women not only made speeches, but actually offered advice to Callirhoe as though she were before them. "Do not give up your girlhood choice; take the man who loved you first, your countryman, so that you may see your father once more. If not, you will live as an exile in a foreign land."

But the other women said, "Choose your benefactor, the man who rescued you, not the one who caused your death. What if Chaereas should get angry again? Will it mean the tomb once more? Do not betray your son. Honor the father of your child."

This was the sort of talk to be heard, so that you might say that all Babylon was a courtroom.

There came the last night before the trial, and the king and queen lay pondering quite different thoughts. The queen prayed for daylight to come more quickly so that she could get rid of her burdensome charge. The fact was that the beauty

85

of the girl, compared so closely with her own, was weighing upon her. Moreover, she felt suspicious of the frequent visits of the king and his untimely compliments. Whereas previously he rarely used to come into the women's quarters, now, since Callirhoe had been there, his visits were continual. She had, moreover, observed him even in the midst of conversation looking indirectly toward Callirhoe, his eyes stealing glances and unconsciously straying in that direction.

So Statira was anticipating the coming day with pleasure; but not so the king. Instead, he remained wakeful throughout all the night, "now lying on his side, now on his back, now on his face," turning matters over in his mind and saying to himself, "The decision is at hand; so hasty I was in granting a short postponement. What are we to do in the morning? In any case Callirhoe will go away, either to Miletus or to Syracuse. Unhappy eyes, you have only a single hour left to enjoy that loveliest of visions; thereafter my slave shall be happier than I. Consider, my soul, what you must do. Return to your normal self. You have no other counselor. Love himself is the lover's counselor.

"First then answer plainly: Who are you, Callirhoe's lover or her judge? Do not deceive yourself. Though you may not know it, you are in love, and there will be all the more proof of this when you can no longer see her. Then, why do you want to cause yourself pain? Your ancestor, the Sun, chose this creature for you, the fairest of those upon whom he looks, and are you going to reject the god's gift?

"Great indeed must be my concern for Chaereas and Dionysius, my humble slaves, to arbitrate their marriage and, Great King that I am, to fulfill the function of an old woman go-between! Yet I volunteered to accept the office of judge and all men know it. Above all, I am ashamed when I think of Statira. Well then, neither advertise your love, nor go through with the trial. It is enough for you just to look at Callirhoe. Postpone the decision. This is possible even for an ordinary jury."

When daylight appeared, the servants made ready the king's courtroom and the people hastened together to the palace and all Babylon was in an uproar. Just as you can see the athletes at the Olympic games arriving at the stadium with their escorting processions, so it was with them too. Dionysius was escorted by the assembled nobility of the Persians, and Chaereas by the common people. There were prayers and countless cheers of encouragement from the supporters of either side, as they shouted, "You are the better man! You will win!" The prize however, was not a wild olive wreath, nor a sheep, nor a pine wreath, but rather the prime of beauty, for which even the gods might justly have contended.

But the king called Artaxates, the eunuch, a highly important person in his sight, and said to him, "According to a dream which came to me, the gods of kings are demanding sacrifice, and I must first fulfill the duties of piety. Proclaim, therefore, a thirty-day festival to be celebrated by all Asia, abandoning both court trials and public business."

The eunuch made the announcement which he had been told to do, and immediately all the land was filled with men offering sacrifice and wearing garlands. There was the sound of the flute and the piping of the syrinx, and the melody of song was heard. Vestibules smoked with incense and every street was a banquet hall, and "the sweet savor arose to heaven eddying amid the smoke." The king set up magnificent sacrifices at the altars, and then for the first time he offered sacrifice to Love as well and called many times upon Aphrodite to help him to favor with her son.

While all were engaged in holiday delights, these three alone were wrapped in grief—Callirhoe, Dionysius, and, most of all, Chaereas. Callirhoe could not openly express her grief in the palace, but quietly and secretly she sighed and uttered imprecations on the festival. Dionysius cursed himself for having ever left Miletus.

"Reckless fool," he said, "you consented to this; now take the consequences. You are yourself to blame. You could have kept Callirhoe, even though Chaereas is alive. You were the master in Miletus and at that time not even the letter could have been given to Callirhoe against your will. Who would have seen her? Who would have approached her? You were in too much haste to rush into the midst of your enemies. And if it were only yourself alone! But as it is, you have jeopardized a possession even more precious than your life. That is why opposition to you has started up on every side. Fool, what do you expect? You have Chaereas as your opponent, and then you make his master your rival, and now the king is seeing visions, and the gods to whom he makes offerings every day are demanding sacrifices from him! The shamelessness of it! While he is dragging out the trial, he is keeping the wife of another man within his palace, and a person of that sort claims to be a judge!"

While Dionysius was lamenting in this fashion, Chaereas refused to touch food and gave up all desire to live. And when his friend Polycharmus sought to prevent him from starving himself to death, he said, "You are my worst enemy under the cloak of friendship! You keep me here in torture and delight to see my punishment. If you were my friend, you would not begrudge me my freedom, persecuted as I am by some evil power. How many times you have destroyed my chances for happiness! How happy I should be if only I had been buried together with Callirhoe at her funeral in Syracuse! But at that time also, though I wanted to die, you prevented me and so robbed me of her sweet companionship. Perhaps then she might not have deserted my corpse and come forth from the tomb. In any case, I should now be lying there, spared my subsequent sufferings—enslavement, pirates, chains, and the king more cruel than the cross. O happy death, that might have come before I heard of the second marriage of Callirhoe!

"And again, after the trial, what an opportunity for ending my sufferings you have ruined! I saw Callirhoe and I did not approach her; I did not kiss her. O strange and unbelievable fact! Chaereas is on trial as to whether he is the husband of Callirhoe! And yet the demon of envy did not permit even this trial, such as it was, to come to completion. Waking and sleeping, the gods truly hate me."

Saying this he rushed for his sword, but Polycharmus held back his hand and, all but putting him in chains, managed to keep watch over him.

The king then summoned his eunuch, who was the most trusted of all his servants, and at first showed some embarrassment even before him. But Artaxates, seeing that he was blushing and wanted to speak, said, "Master, what are you hiding from your servant? I am fond of you and I can hold my tongue. What is this awful thing that has occurred? I am terribly afraid that some plot . . ."

"Yes," said the king, "a very great plot, but one of divine rather than human origin. Long ago I had heard in stories and poems who Love was, and that he was the master over all the gods, including Zeus himself. However, I did not believe that any god could confront me and prove himself more powerful than I. But now here he is. With overpowering violence Love has invaded my heart. It is hard to confess, but I am truly his captive."

As he said this, his eyes filled with tears so that he could add nothing further to his words. In the silence which followed, Artaxates was immediately aware of the origin of his wound. Indeed, even before this he had been somewhat suspicious, and had perceived that the fire was smoldering. Then, besides, there was no doubt or uncertainty that as long as Callirhoe was present, the king could have loved no one else.

Nevertheless he pretended to be in ignorance, and said, "Master, what beauty is there that can overcome your heart, when all that is beautiful is at your command—gold and servants and fine clothing and horses, whole cities and peoples? There are indeed countless beautiful women, but Statira, whom you alone enjoy, is the most beautiful of all women under the sun. Yet the fact of possession puts an end to passion, unless some goddess has descended from heaven above or risen from the sea, like another Thetis. I feel sure that even the gods envy your association with her."

"What you say perhaps is true," replied the king, "that this woman is one of the goddesses; at least her beauty is more than human. Yet she will not admit it, but pretends to be a Greek from Syracuse. This, too, is evidence of her deceit, in that she does not choose to invite embarrassing questions by naming any city subject to us, but rather transports the scene of her story beyond the Ionic Gulf and the great sea. On the pretext of this trial, she has come to vex me, and she it is who has set the stage for the whole drama. But I am surprised that you dared to call Statira the most beautiful of all women when you have seen Callirhoe. Well, we must think up some way to free me from my pain. Look everywhere and see if it is possible to find a remedy."

"Your Majesty," he replied, "this remedy which you seek has already been found among both Greeks and Persians. There is indeed no other remedy for love except the very object of one's love. This is the real meaning of the well-known saying, 'He who caused the wound shall work the cure.' "

The king was much embarrassed at this speech and said, "Do not ever suggest such a thing as that—to seduce the wife of another man. I am mindful of the laws which I myself have imposed, and of the rules of justice which I practice among all men. Do not accuse me of any such lack of control. I have not fallen so low as that."

Fearful of having spoken too boldly, Artaxates changed his tone to one of praise. "Your sentiments, Your Majesty, are noble indeed," he said. "Do not administer to your love the same sort of remedy which other men would use, but rather one more potent and worthy of a king. Struggle against yourself! You and you alone, my master, can win the victory, even over a god. Therefore divert your heart with every sort of pleasure. You are especially fond of hunting. Indeed, I have known you to spend the whole day without food or drink in the delights of the hunt. It is better, then, to spend your time in hunting than to remain in the palace and be close to the fire."

He agreed to this, and an elaborate hunting party was announced. Horsemen rode forth in full array, including the most noble of the Persians and a picked company from the rest of the army. Though they were all worth seeing, the king himself was the most distinguished figure among them. He rode a very fine large Nisaean horse which had a golden bridle and golden cheek-pieces, as well as a frontlet and breast ornaments. The king was dressed in Tyrian purple of Babylonian weave, and wore a turban of hyacinth hue. About his waist was girded a golden dagger, he carried two javelins, and slung about his shoulder was a quiver and bow of the richest Eastern make, and he sat in the saddle majestically. Fondness for adornment is indeed a characteristic of love. His wish was to be seen by Callirhoe in the midst of all, and as he rode out through the whole city, he kept looking about to see if she too perhaps was observing the procession.

Soon the mountains were filled with shouting and running, with barking dogs and whinnying horses and fleeing game. Their excitement and confusion might have routed the god of love himself, for complete delight was there; joy combined with earnest rivalry and the sweetness of risk spiced with terror.

Yet the king did not see a single horse, though so many riders were racing by, nor any beast of all that were being pursued; he heard not one dog amid the baying of so many, nor even the men though all were shouting. He could see only Callirhoe, though she was not there, and could hear only her voice, though she was not speaking. Love had in fact ridden out with him to the hunt, and, since he is a god fond of contention and had seen that the king was opposing him with plans, as he thought, well-laid, Love turned his own device against him, and used the very cure to inflame his heart.

Love entered his mind and said, "How fine it would be to see Callirhoe here, with her dress girt to her knees and her arms uncovered, with flushed face, and heaving bosom. Truly 'even as Artemis the archer, she moveth down the mountain, either along the ridges of lofty Taÿgetus or Erymanthus, taking her pastime in the chase of boars and swift deer'."

Picturing and imagining her thus, the king was greatly inflamed . . .*

While he was uttering these words, Artaxates interrupted and said, "Master, you have forgotten the situation. Callirhoe does not in fact possess a husband, and the trial is still impending to decide whom she ought to marry. Remember, then, it is a widow you love. Therefore do not fear the laws, because they are established to protect marriage, and as for adultery, there must first be a husband who is wronged, and only then an adulterer who does the wrong."

This speech pleased the king, since it suited his inclinations. So, placing his arm about the eunuch, he kissed him and said, "It is only right that I should honor you above all others. You are indeed my kindest friend and noble protector. Go now and bring Callirhoe; but two conditions I impose upon you. Do not do it against her will nor yet openly. I want you to win her over and at the same time to do it secretly."

So at once retreat was sounded for the hunt and they all turned back. The king, now in high hopes, rode back to the palace as pleased as though he had hunted down the noblest game. Artaxates, too, rejoiced in the thought that he had rendered him a true service and that from then on he would hold the reins at court, inasmuch as they both would feel grateful to him, and especially Callirhoe. Like the eunuch and slave and barbarian that he was, he considered the whole matter easy, and had no idea of the noble pride of the Greek and especially of Callirhoe, who was so modest and loyal to her husband.

Thus, waiting his chance, he approached her, and finding her alone, he said, "Lady, I have brought you a perfect treasure-chest of good news. And for your part, don't forget my kindness; I am sure you are not ungrateful."

At the beginning of his speech Callirhoe grew very happy, for people are naturally inclined to believe what they wish. And so she expected that she would soon be restored to Chaereas, and, eager to hear the good news, promised the eunuch his reward.

---

*A sentence or two seems to have been lost at this point.

He then started once more from the beginning and said, "Lady, your fortune lies in your heavenly beauty, and yet you have reaped no really great or important advantage from it. Your great renown may be celebrated over all the earth, but until today it has not gained you a husband or a lover worthy of you. Instead, it has been wasted on two men, one a poor islander, and the other a servant of the king. What great distinction have you derived from them? What fertile lands do you own? What costly jewelry do you possess? Of what states are you queen? How many servants offer homage to you? The women of Babylon have maids that are richer than you! Yet you have not been entirely neglected. The gods are now providing for you; that is why they brought you here, discovering in the trial a pretext for the Great King to look upon you. Here you have the first of my good news. He has looked upon you with pleasure, and I keep reminding him of you and sing your praises in his presence."

This last was his own addition. Indeed every slave, when he talks to anyone concerning his master, always puts in a recommendation for himself as well, seeking personal gain from the conversation.

Callirhoe's heart was struck by this speech as by a sword, but she pretended not to understand, and said, "May the gods continue to be gracious to the king, and he to you, for having taken pity on an unfortunate girl. I beg him to set me free from my anxiety the sooner by concluding the trial, so that I need no longer be a burden to the queen."

The eunuch, thinking that he had failed to express his meaning clearly, and that the girl had not understood, began to speak more plainly. "This is the very essence of your good fortune, that you no longer have slaves and poor men as your lovers, but the Great King instead, who can freely give you Miletus itself and all Ionia and Sicily and other still greater nations. Therefore offer sacrifices to the gods and count yourself happy. Strive to please him still more, and when you attain wealth, remember me."

Callirhoe's first impulse was, if possible, to dig out the eyes of her seducer; but being a well-brought-up and intelligent girl, she at once took into account both where she was and the identity of the speaker in relation to herself. So she restrained her anger and addressed the barbarian with assumed humility.

"May I never be so mad," she said, "as to believe myself worthy of the Great King! Indeed I am no better than the maidservants of the women of Persia. So please do not make any further mention of me to your master. I assure you that even though he may not be angry now, he will deal with you severely later, when he stops to think how you have brought the ruler of the world down to the level of a slave of Dionysius. I am surprised, too, that since you are so intelligent, you fail to recognize the human kindness of the king, and the fact that he is not in love with an unfortunate girl, but rather pities her. Therefore let us stop this idle talk, for fear someone may report us to the queen."

Thereupon she ran away and the eunuch stood there with his mouth open. Brought up as he was in the atmosphere of despotism, he naturally believed that nothing was impossible either for the king or yet for himself. Thus, left alone and denied even the courtesy of an answer, he retired, his heart filled with a number of emotions—anger toward Callirhoe, annoyance at himself, and terror of the king. Indeed it was quite possible that the king would not believe that he had interviewed her at all, albeit unsuccessfully, and he might seem to be betraying his duty to the king while seeking favor with the queen. Also he was much afraid that Callirhoe would report this conversation straight to her, and that Statira in her anger would get him into some serious trouble, on the grounds that he was not only supporting but even promoting the king's passion.

While the eunuch was thus considering how he might report the matter to the king with safety, Callirhoe, as soon as she was herself, exclaimed, "This is what I prophesied, as you can testify, Euphrates! I predicted that I should not again cross your stream. Farewell, father, and you, too, mother, and Syracuse, my native land; I shall not see you again! Now in very truth Callirhoe's death has come. Once I came forth from the tomb, but from here not even the pirate Theron shall lead me out. O treacherous beauty, you are the cause of all my woes! Because of you, I was murdered; because of you, I was sold as a slave; because of you, I was again married after losing Chaereas; because of you, I was brought to Babylon; because of you, I stood before the tribunal. Think of all the ordeals to which you have betrayed me—pirates, the sea, the tomb, slavery, the courtroom! And hardest to bear of all, is the king's love.

"As yet I have not mentioned the anger of the king, for I consider the queen's jealousy still more terrible, which even Chaereas, a man and a Greek, could not withstand. What will she do, woman and barbarian mistress that she is? Come, Callirhoe, decide on some heroic deed, worthy of Hermocrates. Kill yourself! But wait—not yet. So far there is nothing but talk of love heard from a eunuch. If, however, matters take a more violent turn, then is the time to demonstrate your loyalty to Chaereas in his presence."

The eunuch went to the king and tried to conceal the true account of what had happened, and put forth, as his excuse for being unable to approach Callirhoe, lack of time and the need of keeping careful watch on the queen.

"Master," he said, "you ordered me to be careful not to show my hand. You were right in that. You have assumed the most dignified role of judge, and as such you want to keep your high reputation among the Persians. It is on this point that all men praise you. The Greeks, on the other hand, are sticklers, and they love to talk. They will see to it that this affair is well-advertised. Callirhoe will want to boast that the king is her lover, and Dionysius and Chaereas will be impelled by their jealousy. It is not fair, either, to cause pain to the queen, whose reputation for beauty has only been increased by this trial." He tried to introduce this change of tune, hoping he might divert the king from his passion and relieve himself of his burdensome duty.

For the time he did succeed in persuading him, but when night came, the king was again on fire, and Love kept reminding him of those glorious eyes and that beautiful face of Callirhoe. He praised her hair, her walk, her voice, the way she entered the courtroom, the way she stood, the way she spoke, her very silence, her embarrassment, and her weeping. After remaining awake the greater part of the night and sleeping only long enough to see Callirhoe in his dreams as well, he called the eunuch at dawn and said, "Go and keep watch of her all day. You will surely find some opportunity, however brief, for talking with her secretly. Of course I have the guards at my disposal, if I wanted to use open force to satisfy my passion."

With a low bow the eunuch promised his aid, for no one can object when the king commands. He was aware, however, that Callirhoe would give him no opportunity but would deliberately avoid any conversation with him by taking refuge with the queen. So, wishing to take care of this point, he turned the blame from the fugitive upon her protector and said, "Master, if you please, send for Statira and say that you want a private conversation with her. In that way her absence will give me a chance at Callirhoe."

"Do that," said the king.

So Artaxates came and bowed low to the queen. "Mistress," he said, "your husband is calling you."

When Statira heard this, she bowed low and hastened away to him. Then the eunuch, seeing that Callirhoe was left alone, took her right hand, as though he loved the Greeks and all mankind, and led her apart from the group of her servants. She understood his intention, but, though she immediately became pale and speechless, still she followed him.

When they were by themselves, he said to her, "You have seen how the queen bowed low on hearing the name of the king and went off in haste. But you, who are his slave, do not appreciate your good luck, and are not even satisfied to have him invite you, although he could command you. However, I have not betrayed your folly to him, for I do respect you. Instead I have done the opposite; I have made promises to him in your name. That means, there are two paths before you, of which you may take your choice. I will name them both to you. In the one case, if you obey the king, you will receive splendid presents from him and have the husband whom you desire; for, of course, he does not intend to marry you, but you will provide him merely with distraction for the moment. In the other case, whether you want it or not, you will have to endure the fate suffered by the king's enemies—and *they* are not allowed to die, no matter how much they desire it."

Callirhoe laughed at his threat and said, "This will not be the first time that I have suffered horribly. I am well acquainted with misfortune. What can the

93

king devise for me that is worse than what I have already endured? I was buried alive, and the tomb is narrower than any prison; I was delivered into the hands of pirates; and just now I am suffering the greatest of my misfortunes—though Chaereas is here, I cannot see him."

These words of hers betrayed her, for the eunuch, who was naturally shrewd, realized that she was in love.

"You poor, silly girl," he said, "do you prefer the slave of Mithridates to the Great King of Persia?"

Callirhoe was incensed at this slur upon Chaereas and said, "Keep a civil tongue in your head, fellow. Chaereas is noble born. He comes from a city of the first rank, which not even the Athenians could conquer—and they triumphed over your Great King at Marathon and Salamis."

As she said this, she burst into tears. But the eunuch pressed her all the more.

"You yourself are to blame for this delay," he said. "The question is, how to gain the favor of the judge so as to get back your husband, too. It is possible that Chaereas may not even know what you do, and even if he does, he will not be jealous of his superior. He will think you all the more precious for having pleased the king."

This he added not so much for her sake, but because he really believed it. All barbarians, you know, stand in blind awe of a king and consider him to be a god in person. But Callirhoe would not have welcomed marriage even with Zeus himself, nor have preferred even immortality to one day with Chaereas.

So the eunuch, being unable to accomplish his purpose, said, "I will give you time for consideration, my lady. Consider, then, not only your own plight but Chaereas' as well, since he is in danger of a most dreadful death. The king will not endure to be outrivaled in love." And so he went away, but his last remark touched Callirhoe's heart.

But now Fortune quickly brought a change to all reflections and conversations about love and discovered the grounds for still stranger happenings. Messengers who came to the king reported that there was a revolt on a grand scale in Egypt. They said that the Egyptians had put to death the royal governor, and had elected a king from among the natives, and that he had set out from Memphis and had passed through Pelusium and was now overrunning Syria and Phoenicia; that the cities were no longer offering any opposition, but it was as though some raging torrent or great conflagration had rushed down upon them.

At this report the king was greatly disturbed and the Persians were struck with terror. Gloom enveloped all Babylon. Then the soothsayers and prophets of the king declared that his dream had foretold the future; for, they said, to dream of gods demanding sacrifice was a sign of danger, but of victory as well.

Everything was said and done which is customary and natural at the unexpected outbreak of war, and Asia was subject to great commotion. Accordingly the king called together the Persian nobles and the leaders of the other nations who were present, with whom he was wont to discuss affairs of importance, and proceeded to deliberate concerning this turn of events. One man urged one course, and another, another, but all were satisfied that they should make haste and, if possible, not postpone action even for a single day.

There were two reasons for this, first, that they might prevent the enemy from increasing in power, and secondly, that they might inspire more confidence in their friends by showing them that help was near. Indeed, if they delayed, everything would turn to the opposite result; their enemies would scorn them as cowards, and their own men would surrender for lack of support. It was very fortunate for the king, they said, that this news reached him, not in Bactra or in Ecbatana, but rather in Babylon, close to the Syrian border, for, once he had crossed the Euphrates, he would have the rebels in his power. He decided, therefore, to lead out the forces he had already with him, and to send out messengers in every direction to order the whole army to assemble at the Euphrates River.

Now the mobilization of the Persian forces is most easily effected. It is all arranged, originally by Cyrus, the first king of the Persians, just which of the tribes are to send cavalry to battle and how great a number they must supply; also which of them are to send infantry, and how many; likewise who must send archers, and how many chariots apiece, both ordinary and scythe-bearing; where the elephants are to come from, and how many; and also the financial contributors of whatever nature and amount. All these preparations take only as much time as one man would need to get ready.

On the fifth day after the proclamation, the king rode out from Babylon with a general command for all to follow who were of military age. Dionysius also was among those who left the city, since he was an Ionian, and no member of a subject state was permitted to remain behind. Putting on his best armor and forming a respectable band of his followers, he took his place among the first and most conspicuous ranks. It was plain that he intended to perform gallant service, since he was naturally an ambitious man and so far from considering personal bravery unimportant that he valued it among the noblest of virtues. Then, too, on this occasion, he felt some vague hope that if he proved himself useful in battle, he would receive Callirhoe from the king as a reward of his bravery, regardless of the outcome of the trial.

Now the queen had no desire that Callirhoe should be taken along, and for that reason she made no mention of her to the king and did not even inquire what his orders were to do with the stranger. Moreover, Artaxates, too, remained silent, ostensibly because he did not dare to remind his master of this romantic distraction now that he was beset by dangers, but actually because he was as delighted to be

95

rid of her as of a savage beast. Indeed one could well imagine that he felt grateful to this war for having cut short this passion of the king which had been fed by idleness.

However, the king did not forget Callirhoe, and the memory of her beauty haunted him even in the midst of this indescribable confusion, although he was ashamed to say anything about her for fear of appearing so utterly callow as to recall a beautiful girl in the midst of so great a war as this. Thus, while he did not say anything to Statira herself nor yet to the eunuch who shared his romantic secret, still, yielding to the force of his desire, he devised the following plan.

It is the custom for the king and the nobles among the Persians, when they go to war, to take along with them their wives and children, their gold and silver and fine clothing, their eunuchs and mistresses, their dogs and furniture, and all objects of wealth and luxury. Accordingly the king summoned the servant in charge of these matters and at first talked at great length and gave general instructions for the disposal of each object. Then finally he mentioned Callirhoe, with a matter-of-fact expression as though it was of no concern to him.

"As for that little foreign girl," he said, "the one whose case I undertook to judge—see that she follows along with the rest of the women."

And so Callirhoe went out from Babylon not without pleasure, because she expected that Chaereas would be leaving too. In any case, she thought, many and uncertain are the accidents of war and for the unfortunate they include changes for the better; and so, perhaps, the trial too would reach its conclusion there as soon as peace had been restored.

BOOK VII

BOOK VII

DURING the general exodus with the king to the war against the Egyptians, no one issued a summons to Chaereas, because he was not the king's slave, but at that moment the only free person in Babylon. He was glad of this since he supposed that Callirhoe, too, was remaining behind. Thus on the following day he came to the palace in search of his wife. Observing, however, that it was closed, and that a great many guards were at the gates, he wandered about the whole city in his search, and with almost insane persistence he kept asking his friend Polycharmus, "Where is Callirhoe? What has happened to her? Surely she, too, has not joined the expedition!"

When he could not find Callirhoe, he set out to look for Dionysius, his rival, and came to his house; whereupon, as though by coincidence, someone came out and told him what he had been instructed to say. Dionysius had in fact devised this sort of stratagem, desiring that Cheareas should give up all hopes of regaining Callirhoe and no longer wait for the outcome of the trial. When he started out for battle, he had left behind a messenger to tell Chaereas that the Persian king, having need of allies, had sent Dionysius to collect an army against Egypt, and that he had given him Callirhoe to ensure his faithful and zealous service.

Chaereas readily believed what he heard, for a man in misfortune is easily deceived. Accordingly he tore at his clothes and his hair, and, as he beat his breast, he exclaimed, "Faithless Babylon! Cruel host! To me a very desert! What a noble judge! He has become the procurer of another man's wife. A wedding in time of war! And I was carefully preparing my case, sure that I should make a just defense. Now I have lost my case by default, and Dionysius has won without saying a word. But his victory shall do him no good. Callirhoe will not live, kept from Chaereas when she knows he is near, even though at first he may have deceived her by pretending I was dead. Then why do I hesitate? Why not cut my throat in front of the palace and pour forth my blood at the very gates of my judge? Let the Persians and the Medes know what kind of justice their king has rendered here!"

Polycharmus, seeing that he could bring no comfort in this disaster, and that it was impossible to save Chaereas, said, "My dearest friend, in the past I have tried to comfort you, and many times I have prevented your death, but now I think your decision is right. And so far am I from preventing you that now I, too, am ready to meet death with you. However, we should consider what sort of death may be best. The one which you propose may bring some reproach on the king and some sense of shame for the future, but it will not amount to much of a revenge for our sufferings. I think that whatever death we have once determined on, we should use to bring punishment to this tyrant. It will be a fine thing indeed to cause him pain and bring him to true repentance, and to bequeath to future generations the glorious tale of two Greeks who suffered injustice and brought painful retribution upon the Great King and died like men."

"But," said Chaereas, "we are only two men, poor and strangers here. How can we do any damage to the lord of all these powerful nations? We have seen the resources which he possesses. He has bodyguards and sentinels, and even if we do succeed in killing some one of his men or in setting fire to some of his property, he will not even notice the damage."

"What you say would be true," said Polycharmus, "if there were no war; but now, as we hear, Egypt has revolted, Phoenicia has been captured, and Syria is being overrun. The enemy will meet the king even before he crosses the Euphrates. Therefore we are not two men alone. Rather we have as many allies as the Egyptian leader commands, and all his arms, resources, and ships. Let us use the strength of others to effect our own vengeance."

While the words were yet on his lips Chaereas shouted, "Hurry! Let us go! I shall get justice in war from this judge of mine."

They set out in haste and pursued the king, under the pretense of wanting to join his forces, since by this device they hoped to cross the Euphrates without danger. They came upon the army at the river bank, and joined in with the rear guard and followed along. Once they had arrived in Syria, however, they deserted to the Egyptians.

The Egyptian guards seized them and inquired who they were, for the fact that they were not dressed as official emissaries aroused suspicions that they were probably spies. On this point they would have incurred great danger, had there not happened to be a Greek at hand, who understood their speech. They demanded to be brought before the Egyptian king, declaring that they had a proposal greatly to his advantage.

When they were brought in, Chaereas said, "We are Greeks and belong to the first families in Syracuse. My friend here came to Babylon for my sake, and I came for the sake of my wife who is the daughter of Hermocrates—in case you have heard of Hermocrates, the general who defeated the Athenians on the sea."

The Egyptian nodded, for there was no nation on earth which had not heard of the disaster which the Athenians suffered in the Sicilian war.

"Artaxerxes has used us cruelly," they said, and told him the whole story. "So of our own accord we are offering ourselves to you as your true friends. We have the two greatest incentives to bravery, desire for death and love of revenge. Indeed, so far as my misfortunes are concerned, I might as well be dead, and hereafter I live only to bring pain to my enemy. 'At least let me not die without a struggle or ingloriously, but in some great deed of arms whereof men yet to be born shall hear.'"

The Egyptian was delighted to hear this and held out his hand and said, "Young man, you have come at just the right time for both of us."

Then he ordered armor and a tent to be given them immediately. Not long afterwards he made Chaereas first his messmate, and then his adviser, such was the intelligence and courage which he demonstrated; besides this, he inspired confidence as a man of good parts with more than a smattering of education. Then, too, his enmity toward the Persian king and his desire to show that he was not lightly to be despised, but worthy of respect, increased his efforts still more and made him yet more prominent. Very soon, in fact, he displayed his ability by a remarkable achievement.

The Egyptian campaign had in general moved forward with ease. The king had become master of Coele Syria as a result of his raid upon it, and Phoenicia, too, surrendered to him with the exception of Tyre. The Tyrians, however, are by nature a most warlike race who seek to maintain a reputation for bravery so as to avoid the appearance of disgracing the god Heracles, who is their most prominent divinity, and to whom they have dedicated their city almost exclusively. Likewise the way their city is built gives them an added sense of security. It is actually built right in the sea with only a narrow approach to unite it to the shore and to keep it from being an island. It is like a ship at anchor with the gangplank resting upon land. Thus it is easy for them to shut out an enemy from any direction; they can keep off a land force by their position in the sea, since they need only a single gate, and they can keep off the attack of war vessels by their walls, since the city is stoutly fortified and is locked by its surrounding harbors tight as a house.

Thus, when all the surrounding peoples had been captured, the Tyrians alone defied the Egyptians and preserved their loyalty and good faith to the Persian king. Vexed at this, the Egyptian summoned his council and then for the first time he invited Chaereas to take part in their deliberations.

"You are my allies, gentlemen," said he, "and I would not think of calling my friends 'servants.' You perceive our difficulties. Like a ship, we have long enjoyed smooth sailing, but now we are caught by a contrary wind, and it is the city of Tyre, an ill wind indeed, which has checked our progress. Also the Persian king is close at our heels, as we have learned. What, then, must we do? It is not possible to capture Tyre, nor yet to pass beyond it. It lies like a wall in our path and shuts us off from all Asia. I think we had best withdraw from here as rapidly as possible, before the Persian force joins with the Tyrians. It is dangerous for us to be caught on enemy soil. Pelusium is strongly fortified and there we need have no fear of Tyrians or Medes or any one else who may come against us. The desert sand there is impassable, the approach is narrow, the sea is ours, and the river Nile is the friend of the Egyptian."

At these overcautious words, they all stood silent and dejected. Only Chaereas dared to speak.

"Your Majesty," said he, "—for so I can truly call you rather than that arch-criminal of Persia—it pains me to hear you considering flight on the very eve of victory. If the gods consent, we shall win, and we shall capture not only Tyre, but Babylon as well. Many obstacles arise in war, but we must in no wise hesitate to face them, but rather set to work, keeping ever before our eyes the expectation of success. As for these Tyrians who now hold us in scorn, I shall bring them before you stripped and in chains. If you do not believe me, then kill me first before you go, for so long as I am alive, I shall refuse to share your flight. If you will go in any case, then leave a few volunteers to stay with me. Like Homer's heroes, yet will we twain, even I and Polycharmus, fight, for in God's name are we come."

For very shame they all supported Chaereas in his sentiments, and the king, astonished at his bold spirit, gave him permission to take as large a body of picked soldiers as he wished. However, he did not choose them immediately, but joining the throng in the camp and bidding Polycharmus to do likewise, he first tried to find out whether there were any Greeks at hand. Sure enough, several were found serving as mercenaries, and from these he selected some Spartans and Corinthians and the rest of the Peloponnesians. He discovered also about twenty Sicilians.

Having thus made up a band of three hundred men, he addressed them as follows: "Fellow Greeks, when the king gave me the authority to select the best soldiers in the army, I chose you. I, too, am a Greek, you see. I come from Syracuse, and am of Dorian stock. It is our duty to prove our superiority to the rest not only in our noble ancestry but by our courage as well. So no one need be alarmed at this business which I am calling on you to undertake; indeed, we shall find it both possible and easy, and more difficult in appearance than in fact. This same number of Greeks once stood up against Xerxes at Thermopylae. The Tyrians, however, are no half-million in number, but only a few, and they rely upon their impudence and bragging, not upon courage and good sense. Let us make them realize the great difference between Greeks and Phoenicians.

"Now I have no desire to be your general, but I am ready to follow any man of you who may wish to hold command. He will find me obedient, since my ambition is not for personal glory but for the common glory of us all."

At this they all shouted, "You must be our general!"

"Since you wish it," he said, "I will be your general, and this supreme command is your gift to me. For that reason I shall make every effort to see that you do not regret having conferred this mark of favor and confidence upon me. Indeed with God's help you shall gain present glory and fame as well as the greatest wealth among the allies, and, for the future, you shall leave behind an undying memory of your heroism. Just as men shall sing of the deeds of the 'noble three hundred' with Miltiades or Leonidas, so, too, they all shall celebrate the comrades of Chaereas."

Before he had finished, they all shouted, "Lead us on," and rushed for their arms.

Chaereas then equipped them with the best possible armor and led them to headquarters. The king on seeing them was astonished, and imagined that instead of his familiar troops he must be looking at strangers, and he promised them large rewards.

"We are sure of that," said Chaereas, "but you must keep the rest of the army under arms and not attack Tyre until we have gained possession of it and have climbed on the walls and called you."

"Heaven grant you success," said he.

Accordingly Chaereas led his men against Tyre, keeping them closely massed so that their numbers seemed much smaller; thus actually "buckler pressed on buckler, helm on helm, and man on man." At first they were not observed by the enemy, but when they came near, those who saw them from the walls gave a signal to those inside, though the last thing in the world they expected was that they were enemies. Indeed, who could have guessed that so small a number was coming to attack this extremely powerful city, against which not even the entire forces of Egypt had ever had the courage to advance? Instead, when they were getting close to the walls, they were asked who they were and what they wanted.

"We are Greek mercenaries," replied Chaereas, "who have failed to receive our pay from the Egyptians, and being threatened with death as well, we have come to you wishing to revenge ourselves with you upon our common foe."

This was reported to those inside and the commanding officer opened the gates and came out with a few men. Chaereas killed him first and rushed upon the others, and he "smote them right and left and there rose a hideous moaning." Each picked his man for slaughter, like lions who fall on an unguarded herd of cattle. Groaning and wailing prevailed throughout the city, for, though few saw what was taking place, they all were thrown into confusion. A disorderly crowd poured out through the gate, wanting to see what had happened. It was this which sealed the doom of the Tyrians. While those on the inside were forcing their way out, those outside, struck and pierced with swords and spears, were trying to escape inside again. The result was that they met each other at the narrow entrance, and offered an excellent opportunity to their attackers; furthermore, it was no longer possible to shut the gates since the corpses were piled so high there.

In this indescribable confusion Chaereas alone kept calm. Forcing back those who met them and gaining the inside of the gate, he and nine others leaped upon the walls and from above gave the signal to call the Egyptians. In less time than it takes to tell they arrived, and so Tyre was captured.

While all the others were celebrating the capture of Tyre, Chaereas alone refused either to offer a sacrifice or to wear a garland.

"What good are celebrations of victory to me," he said, "if you, Callirhoe, cannot see them? In memory of that wedding night of ours, I shall never wear a garland again. If you are dead, it shows lack of respect, and even if you are living, how can I join the feast even in such circumstances as these, when I must take my place apart from you?"

Meantime the Persian king had crossed the Euphrates and was hurrying to engage with the enemy as quickly as possible. When he learned that Tyre was captured, he became anxious about the fate of Sidon and of Syria in general, seeing that the enemy was already proving to be a match for him. Therefore he decided no longer to travel with all his retinue but to advance in lighter marching order, so that there might be no impediment to his speed. Accordingly he took with him the soundest portion of his army, and left behind those of unserviceable age with the queen, as well as the provisions, clothing, and royal treasure. And since everything seemed to be full of alarm and confusion and the cities clear to the Euphrates were in the throes of war, he thought it safer to put those whom he was leaving behind out of danger in Aradus.

Now Aradus is an island about three miles from the mainland, which contains an ancient shrine of Aphrodite. There the women passed the time in complete security, as though at home. Callirhoe observed the statue of Aphrodite and took her stand opposite it. At first she remained silent and wept, reproaching the goddess with her tears. Then with difficulty she uttered these words:

"So now it is Aradus, a tiny island compared with mighty Sicily, and not a friend do I have here! Mistress, this is enough! How long wilt thou treat me as thine enemy? Even though I have greatly offended thee, thou hast had thy revenge. Though my wretched beauty aroused thine indignation, still it has been the cause of my ruin. Now I have experienced that one misfortune which was still left for me—war. Compared to my present state, even Babylon was kindly; there at any rate Chaereas was near me. But now certainly he is dead; he could not have survived after I had gone away. Yet I have no one to ask what has happened to him. All are strangers, all are barbarians who are jealous of me and hate me; and those who love me are worse than those who hate me! Do thou, mistress, tell me plainly if Chaereas still lives."

With these words on her lips she went away. She was overheard by Rhodogyne, the daughter of Zopyrus and the wife of Megabyzus, whose father and husband both were Persian nobles. She it was of the Persian women who first met Callirhoe when she entered Babylon.

When the Egyptian heard that the Persian king was near and had made his preparations for attack by both land and sea, he called Chaereas and said, "I have not had a chance to reward you for your first success in delivering Tyre into my hands. But as for what comes next, only see to it, please, that we do not lose our present advantages, and I shall give you your share. Egypt will be enough for me, and you shall have Syria for your own. Come, now, let us consider what to do. The war is reaching its climax on both land and sea. I offer you your choice, either to command the infantry, if you wish, or the fleet. I believe, however, that the sea is more appropriate for you, for it was you Syracusans who defeated even the Athenians on the sea. Today your opponents will be the Persians who were once defeated by the Athenians. You have Egyptian war vessels which are larger and more numerous than those of the Sicilians. Imitate the prowess of your kinsman, Hermocrates, on the sea."

"Any risk is sweet to me," Chaereas replied. "To serve you I will undertake this campaign against the king, whom in any case I hate most bitterly. But together with the war vessels give me my three hundred soldiers also."

"Take them and as many others as you wish," he said. This was no sooner said than done, for the need was pressing.

Thus the Egyptian went out to engage the enemy with the infantry, while Chaereas was appointed admiral of the fleet. At first, the infantry became somewhat dispirited to think that Chaereas was not to take the field with them, for by now they had great affection for him, and were hopeful of success under his leadership, so that losing him seemed like taking the eye from some unwieldy creature. The fleet, on the other hand, was exalted with hopes and filled with courage because now it had its bravest and noblest leader. Their resolves were anything but half-hearted; instead, captains and pilots and sailors and marines alike, all set out to see who should be first to demonstrate his zeal to Chaereas.

On the same day battle was joined both on land and on sea. The Egyptian infantry held out a long time against the Medes and Persians, and then, overwhelmed by superior numbers, they gave in and the Great King came riding in pursuit. There was an earnest effort on the part of the Egyptian to take refuge in Pelusium, while the Persian was eager to catch up with him first. He might perhaps have escaped, too, if it had not been for a remarkable performance exhibited by Dionysius.

Even in the first encounter he had fought brilliantly, always engaging in action near the king so as to be seen by him, and he was the first to rout the enemy opposite him. Then, later, when the retreat was prolonged successively through some days and nights, he saw that the king was distressed at this, and said, "Do not worry, Sire; I shall prevent the Egyptian from escaping if you will give me some picked cavalrymen."

The king approved, and gave them to him. Then with five thousand of them, he completed two days' journey in a single day, and falling upon the Egyptians unexpectedly by night, captured many of them, and slaughtered more. The Egyptian king though captured alive, killed himself, and Dionysius brought his head to the Great King.

On seeing it, the latter said, "I am enrolling you as a benefactor to my house, and right now I grant you the sweetest of gifts, and one which you especially desire above all others—Callirhoe, as your wife. War has handed down the decision. You have the fairest prize for your valor."

Dionysius bowed low and considered himself as an equal of the gods, convinced that now surely he was the husband of Callirhoe.

So much for what took place on land. On the sea Chaereas was so victorious that the enemies' fleet did not even stand up against him. They could neither sustain the ramming of the Egyptian vessels nor face them at all prow to prow. Instead, some were immediately turned back, and others were forced ashore, and captured, crews and all. The sea was filled with the wreckage of Persian ships. Yet the king was not aware of the defeat of his forces on the sea, nor was Chaereas of the defeat of the Egyptians on the land, but each of them thought that he had the upper hand on both elements.

So, on the same day on which the battle was fought Chaereas sailed down to Aradus and gave orders to circle about the island and to keep it under observation. . . . *with the intention that they should give a report to their master. Likewise they collected the eunuchs, the maidservants, and all the less valuable slaves into the market place, since there was plenty of room there. Indeed, so great was the crowd that they spent the night not only under the porticos, but even under the open sky. Those who had some special value were brought into a building in the market place in which the officials usually transacted business. The women sat around the queen on the ground and neither lighted a fire nor tasted of food, convinced as they were that the king had been captured, that Persia's cause was lost, and that the Egyptian was universally victorious.

During that night Aradus was in the throes at once of greatest delight and deepest dismay. The Egyptians were rejoicing in their deliverance from war and Persian domination, while the captured Persians were in expectation of chains and whips, insults and death, or, at the very mildest, slavery. Statira was weeping with her head resting in Callirhoe's lap. Indeed, the latter could best comfort the queen, since she was a cultured Greek lady with no small experience in misfortune.

Then a remarkable thing happened. An Egyptian soldier who had been entrusted with keeping watch over the occupants of the building, though he knew

*A passage describing the actual capture of Aradus has been lost from the text here.

that the queen was inside, yet did not dare to approach too close because of the inborn servility which barbarians feel at the name of royalty. Instead, he stood by the closed door and said, "Take courage, Your Majesty! Though now the admiral does not know that you too are imprisoned here among the captives, still when he does learn of it, he will look out for you with all kindness. He is not only a brave man but also . . ." *

" . . . he will make you his wife, for he is very chivalrous by nature."

On hearing this, Callirhoe uttered a loud cry of grief and tearing her hair, she said, "Now I really am a prisoner! Kill me rather than bring me a message like this! I will not submit to marriage. I pray rather for death. They can goad me and burn me. I will not get up from here. This place shall be my tomb. If, as you say, your leader is a kindly man, let him grant me this favor; let him kill me right here!"

Once more he forced his demands upon her, but she refused to get up, and, covering her head, she sank to the ground and lay there. The Egyptian was confronted with the problem what he should do. He did not dare to apply force, and he was unable to persuade her; he therefore turned away and came with gloomy face to Chaereas.

On seeing him, the latter said, "This must be something new. Are there some thieves after our best spoils? Well, they'll be sorry for it if they are!"

"There is no harm done, master," replied the Egyptian. "Only, that woman, whom I found sticking to her post like the heroes at Plataea, is unwilling to come, and has thrown herself on the ground, demanding a sword and determined to die."

Chaereas laughed and said, "You are a perfect simpleton! Don't you know how a woman is managed? You must appeal to her, flatter her, and make her promises; especially so if she thinks some one is in love with her. You probably used force and insults."

"Not at all, master," said he, "I tried everything that you mention in double measure. I even lied to her and said that you would take her as your wife. She was particularly annoyed at that."

"I must be a very fascinating and charming person indeed," said Chaereas, "if she has rejected me and hates me even before she has seen me. There seems to be a proud spirit in this woman which is rather noble. See that no one uses violence upon her, but let her carry on as she herself has chosen. I must respect her modesty. Perhaps she, too, is mourning for her husband."

---

*A rather extensive gap in the Greek text, perhaps a page in length, occurs at this point.

BOOK VIII

BOOK VIII

I N THE previous book we have narrated the suspicions of Chaereas that Callirhoe had been given over to Dionysius, his desire for vengeance on the
Persian king and consequent desertion to the king of Egypt, his appointment
as admiral, his mastery of the sea, and his victorious capture of Aradus, where the
king of Persia had hidden away not only his queen and all her attendants, but
Callirhoe as well.

But Fortune's next move was to bring about a situation at once paradoxical
and melancholy. Thereby Chaereas, though in actual possession of Callirhoe, was
not to be aware of the fact, but was to take on board his vessels the wives of other
men and bring them away and leave his own wife there alone—and that, too, not
like the sleeping Ariadne, to be the bride of a Dionysus, but as the spoil of his
own enemies.

However, this seemed outrageous to Aphrodite, who, though she had previously been terribly angered at Chaereas' uncalled-for jealousy, whereby he had
insolently rejected her kindness after receiving from her a gift more superlatively
beautiful even than Paris' prize, was by now becoming reconciled with him. And
since Chaereas had now nobly redeemed himself in the eyes of Love by his wanderings from west to east amid countless sufferings, Aphrodite felt pity for him,
and, as she had in the beginning brought together this noble pair, so now, having
harried them long over land and sea, she was willing once more to unite them.

Furthermore, I think that this last book will be the most pleasant of all to my
readers, and in fact will serve as an antidote to the tragic events of the former ones.
No more piracy or slavery or court trials or battles or suicide or war or capture
here, but true love and lawful marriage! And so I am going to tell you how the
goddess brought the truth to light and revealed the unsuspecting lovers to each
other.

It was evening, but a large amount of the captured material was still left on
shore. Wearied as he was, Chaereas got up to give his orders for embarking. As he
passed by the market place, the Egyptian said, "Master, here is that woman who re-

fuses to come to you, but is determined on suicide. Perhaps you can persuade her to get up, for surely there is no reason why you should leave behind the most beautiful of your prizes."

Polycharmus, too, joined in with this suggestion, since he wished, if possible, to interest Chaereas in a new love so as to comfort him for the loss of Callirhoe.

"Let us go inside and see, Chaereas," he said.

So he crossed the threshold and saw her lying prostrate with her head covered. At once her way of breathing and her general appearance brought a thrill to his heart and he became vaguely excited. Indeed, he certainly would have recognized her, if he had not been so thoroughly convinced that Dionysius had taken Callirhoe away. Quietly approaching her, he said, "My dear, whoever you are, take courage! We are not going to use force on you. You shall have the husband that you want."

While he was still speaking, Callirhoe recognized his voice and uncovered her face. Simultaneously they shrieked: "Chaereas!" "Callirhoe!"

As they rushed into each other's arms they fainted and fell to the floor.

At first Polycharmus, too, stood speechless at this miracle, but after some time had elapsed, he said, "Stand up! You have recovered each other; Heaven has fulfilled the prayers of you both. But remember, you are not at home, but in an enemy country, and first you must manage things carefully so as to prevent any one from separating you again."

This he uttered in loud tones, and they, like people sunk in a deep well, who can barely hear a voice calling from above, slowly recovered. Then, gazing at each other and kissing each other, again they were overcome, and this happened a second and a third time. The only thing they could say was, "Are you really Callirhoe —really Chaereas—whom I hold in my arms?"

The rumor spread that the admiral had found his wife. Not a soldier remained in his tent, nor a sailor on his ship, nor a doorkeeper at his post, but from all sides they flocked together exclaiming, "How happy she must be to have recovered so handsome a husband!" Nevertheless when Callirhoe appeared, no one any longer praised Chaereas, but all turned their gaze toward her, as though she were there alone. She advanced with dignity, Chaereas and Polycharmus escorting her on either side. Flowers and wreaths were cast before them; wine and myrrh were poured at their feet, and the sweetest fruits of war and of peace, the triumph and the wedding, were there combined.

It was Chaereas' custom to sleep on board the warship, busy as he was both night and day. Now, however, he turned everything over to Polycharmus, and as for himself did not even wait until evening before coming to the royal apartments; in every city, you know, a special house is set aside for the use of the Great King. A couch of beaten gold was placed there, and its covering was Tyrian purple of Babylonian weave.

Who could describe the events of that night—the many stories with which it was filled, the frequent tears and kisses? Callirhoe first began her story—how she had revived in the tomb, how she had been brought out of it by Theron, how she had sailed away, and how she had been sold into slavery. Up to this point Chaereas listened in tears, but when in her narrative she came to Miletus, Callirhoe fell silent with embarrassment, and Chaereas felt the stirrings of his natural jealousy. However, the story of the child comforted him.

Not waiting to hear everything, he said, "Tell me how you came to Aradus, and where you left Dionysius, and what dealings you have had with the king."

She immediately swore that she had not seen Dionysius after the trial. The king, she said, was in love with her, but she had had nothing to do with him, not even a kiss.

"Then," said Chaereas, "I was unjust and too quick-tempered, in treating the king so badly when he had done no harm to you. You see, when I parted from you, I felt myself obliged to desert from him. But I have brought no shame upon you. I have filled land and sea with my triumphs," and he gave her an exact account of it all, priding himself on his accomplishments. When they had had their fill of tears and story-telling, embracing each other, "they came gladly to the rites of their bed, as of old."

While it was still night, an Egyptian of considerable rank sailed in and, stepping ashore from his vessel, eagerly inquired where Chaereas was. When he was brought to Polycharmus, he declared that he could tell his secret mission to no one else, but that the crisis which brought his coming was a pressing one. For some time Polycharmus kept putting off his interview with Chaereas, unwilling to disturb him at an unseasonable time, but when the fellow kept insisting, he opened the door of the chamber a crack, and informed Chaereas of the emergency.

Like a good general, Chaereas said, "Call him in; war will not permit of delays."

When the Egyptian had been brought in—it was still dark—he stood by the bed and said, "You must know that the Persian king has killed the king of Egypt, and has dispatched a portion of his army into Egypt to establish control there. All the rest he is leading in this direction, and is all but here. You see, he has learned that Aradus has been captured, and so is not only worrying about all his wealth which he has left here, but is most specially distressed about the safety of his queen, Statira."

On hearing this Chaereas started to his feet; but Callirhoe, laying her hand upon him, said, "Where are you going in such a hurry? First, carefully consider the situation. If you make this news public, you will stir up serious opposition against yourself; and when people realize the facts, they will all despise you. And if we get into his hands for the second time, our sufferings will be more severe than those we experienced before."

113

Chaereas was quickly convinced by her advice, and came out from the chamber ready with his scheme. Taking the Egyptian by the hand, he called together his whole company and said, "Men, we are victorious over the land forces of the king as well. This man has brought us the good news together with letters from the Egyptian king, and we must set sail as soon as possible to the place to which he has ordered us. So make your preparations, all of you, and get on board."

At these words of his, the trumpeter sounded the recall to the boats. During the previous day, they had put on board the booty and the prisoners, and nothing was left on the island except what was useless or too heavy to move. Then they proceeded to unfasten the stern cables and weigh the anchors, and the harbor was filled with shouting and confusion as each performed his task. Chaereas passed from one trireme to another and gave private orders to the captain of each to set his course toward Cyprus, on the pretext that they had to capture that island while it was still unguarded. Meeting with a favorable breeze, on the following day they put in at Paphos where the temple of Aphrodite is situated.

When they had anchored there, and before anyone had disembarked from the vessels, Chaereas first dispatched the heralds to proclaim peace and a truce to the inhabitants; after their acceptance, he put his whole force on shore, and proceeded to do honor to Aphrodite with offerings. Then, collecting a large number of sacrificial animals, he prepared a feast for his whole company.

While he was considering what to do next, the priests, who are also prophets, reported that the omens of sacrifice were good. This gave him courage, and he summoned the captains of the vessels, his three hundred Greeks, and all the Egyptians who he saw were kindly disposed to himself, and spoke as follows:

"Fellow soldiers and friends, you have shared in our great accomplishments. For my part, I consider that peace is at its best and war at its safest in your company; indeed, we have learned by experience that, being of one mind, we could gain mastery of the sea. But the crucial moment has arrived for us to consider what we shall do for our future safety. The fact is that the king of Egypt has been killed in battle and the Persian is in control of all the land, while we have been cut off in the midst of enemies. Such being the case, is there anyone here who advises us to go over to the king and to throw ourselves unreservedly into his hands?"

They all shouted immediately that anything was better to do than that.

"Then where shall we go? Every circumstance is hostile to us; it is no longer feasible even to put our trust in the sea, now that the land is in the power of our enemies; and obviously we can't fly away!"

In the ensuing silence, a man from Lacedaemon, who was a kinsman of Brasidas and had been exiled from Sparta at a time of great stress, was the first who dared to speak.

"Why are we looking for some place to escape from the king?" he said. "We have got the sea here and our warships, haven't we? They will bring us to Sicily and to Syracuse, where we have no need to fear either the Persians, nor yet the Athenians themselves."

They all applauded this speech. Chaereas alone pretended not to agree; he professed that the journey was too long, but actually he wanted to test the steadfastness of their purpose.

When they strongly insisted and were eager to sail at once, he said, "Fellow Greeks, as for yourselves, your advice is good, and I thank you for your kindness and loyalty; I will not permit you ever to repent of it, if the gods take you under their care. But as for the Egyptians, there are many of them whom it is not proper to force against their will, since the majority of them have wives and children from whom they would not care to be parted. So you must distribute yourselves among their group and be careful to ask each one of them, to make sure that we take with us only those who are willing."

This was done as he had directed. Callirhoe, however, took Chaereas' hand and, leading him off to one side, she said, "What is your intention, Chaereas? Are you also going to take Statira and the beautiful Rhodogyne to Syracuse?"

Chaereas blushed and said, "It is not for my sake that I am taking them, but as servants for you."

"May Heaven never afflict me with such insanity," cried Callirhoe, "as to keep the queen of Asia as my slave, especially when she has been my friend! But if you wish to please me, send her back to the king. It was she, you know, who kept me safe for you, taking me under her protection as though I were her sister-in-law."

"There is nothing," Chaereas replied, "which I would not do if you wanted it. Indeed, you are mistress of Statira and of all the prizes I have won, and, above all else, the mistress of my heart!"

Callirhoe was delighted and kissed him. Then immediately she ordered her servants to take her to Statira.

The latter, as it happened, was in the hold of the ship with the most prominent of the Persian women. She had not the slightest knowledge of what had taken place, not even that Callirhoe had recovered Chaereas, since close guard was kept and no one was permitted to approach her or see her or bring her any report of what was happening. So, when Callirhoe came on board under the escort of the captain, at once they were all struck with astonishment and milled about in confusion; then one remarked softly to another, "The admiral's wife has come."

Statira sighed loudly and deeply. "Fortune," she said, with tears in her eyes, "thou hast preserved me until this day, so that I, a queen, may look upon my mistress! She has probably come to see what sort of a slave she has acquired."

Thereupon she started rocking and moaning with grief, and came at length to realize what captivity means for persons of noble birth.

But Fortune brought a quick change of circumstances. Callirhoe ran in and embraced Statira. "Your Majesty!" she said, "you are a queen, indeed, and you shall always remain one. You have not fallen into the hands of enemies, but rather of your dearest friend whom once you treated so kindly. My Chaereas is admiral; and the thing that made him admiral of the Egyptians was his resentment toward the king for delaying his recovery of me. But that is over now, reconciliation has come, and he is no longer your enemy. So get up now, dearest, and go on your way in happiness. You, too, shall get back your husband. The king is alive and Chaereas is sending you to him. You, too, Rhodogyne, my first friend among the Persians, get up and go home to your husband. So too with all the others the queen may wish, and don't forget Callirhoe."

Statira was overwhelmed on hearing these words and could neither believe them nor disbelieve them. Callirhoe's nature, however, was not such as to give the impression that at so great a crisis she was speaking insincerely. Moreover, their critical situation demanded immediate action.

Now among the Egyptians, there was a certain Demetrius, who was a philosopher and an acquaintance of the king, advanced in years and the superior of the other Egyptians in education and general excellence. Chaereas summoned him and said, "I had intended to take you with me, but instead I will make you my agent on an important business; I am going to send the queen back to the great king with your help. This will at once put you in greater esteem in his sight and will restore the others to his favor."

With these words, he appointed Demetrius the commander of the vessels which were being sent back.

Everyone wanted to follow along with Chaereas, and thought more of him than of their homes and their children. However, he selected twenty vessels only, the largest and the best, intending to make the passage across the Ionic Gulf, and on board them he placed all the Greeks that were there, and all the Egyptians and Phoenicians who he knew were active and unencumbered. Many of the men from Cyprus, too, went on board as volunteers. All the rest he sent to their homes, distributing among them their share of the booty, so that each could return to his family well satisfied with the honors he had received. Not a man failed to be granted any request he made of Chaereas.

Callirhoe brought all her royal adornments to Statira. The latter, however, was unwilling to accept them, but said, "Put them on yourself; royal adornments are suited for beauty such as yours. You must keep them to please your mother and to offer to your ancestral gods. I have more than these, left behind in Babylon. Heaven give you a happy voyage and a safe return, and may you never again be parted from your Chaereas. In every way you have treated me fairly. You have shown a noble nature, one that is worthy of your beauty. It was a happy sponsorship indeed which the king intrusted to me."

Who could describe that day, with its many and varied occupations? Men were praying, making parting agreements, rejoicing, grieving, giving commands one to the other, and writing letters home. Chaereas, too, wrote this letter to the king:

You were intending to decide my case, but I have already won before the most impartial judge of all; for war is the best judge of both better and worse. It has restored Callirhoe to me, and not only my wife, but your wife, too. I have not imitated your slowness, but at once, and even before you ask it, I am restoring Statira to you, unharmed and still a queen, even in captivity; but I want you to know that it is not I who am sending this gift to you, but Callirhoe. One favor we ask you in return; make peace with the Egyptians, since it suits a king above all other men not to hold rancor. You will have good soldiers, who love you, for rather than follow me they have preferred, as your friends, to stay in your service.

Such was Chaereas' letter. And Callirhoe, too, felt that it was only fair and gracious to write to Dionysius. This was the one thing which she did apart from Chaereas, inasmuch as she was aware of his natural jealousy, and so took pains to act without his knowledge. Taking a writing tablet, she inscribed upon it as follows:

Callirhoe to her benefactor, Dionysius, greeting. You are the one who set me free from pirates and from slavery. Please, do not be angry. Indeed, I am with you in spirit because of the son whom we share, and I am intrusting him to you to bring up and to educate in a way worthy of us. Take no chances with a stepmother. You have not only a son, but a daughter as well; two children are enough. When he becomes a man, marry them to each other and send him to Syracuse so that he may see his grandfather, too. My greetings to you, Plangon. This I have written with my own hand. Farewell, good Dionysius, and remember your Callirhoe.

Sealing the letter, she hid it away in her bosom, and when the inevitable hour of sailing came, and every one had to embark, she personally offered her hand to Statira and brought her on board the boat. Demetrius had prepared a royal canopy for her on the vessel, surrounding it with Babylonian tapestries of purple and gold thread. Escorting her deferentially to the couch within, Callirhoe said, "Good-bye, Statira. Remember me and write me often at Syracuse. All things are easy for royalty, you know. I shall acknowledge my gratitude to you before my parents and the gods of Greece. I commend my child to your care, since you, too, were fond of him. Think of him as a sacred trust which you have to take my place."

At these words Statira's eyes filled with tears and the women were moved to lamentation. Then, as she was about to leave the vessel, Callirhoe leaned over towards Statira unobtrusively, and blushing, handed her the letter, saying, "Give this letter to my poor Dionysius; I trust him to your care and to that of the king. Comfort him. I am afraid that he may kill himself now that he has been parted from me."

The women might still be talking and weeping and kissing each other, if the pilots had not given the signal for putting to sea. As Callirhoe was about to go on board, she offered salutation to Aphrodite.

"Mistress," she said, "I thank thee for my present blessings. Now thou art reconciled with me; but grant me, I pray, also to see Syracuse. Mighty is the sea that lies between and the awesome deep awaits me; but I do not fear, if thou wilt sail with me."

Moreover, not one of the Egyptians got on board the vessels of Demetrius without first having said good-by to Chaereas, and having kissed him on cheek and hand; so great affection had he inspired in them all. And at first he permitted the whole fleet to start the voyage in company, so that they could hear each other's cheers commingled with prayers until they were far at sea.

And so they sailed away. But the Great King, after mastering his foes, sent an agent to Egypt to restore matters there to security, while he himself hurried on to see his queen at Aradus. And when he was in the district round about Ijon and Tyre, and was offering sacrifices to Heracles in gratitude for his victory, a messenger came up and reported, "Aradus has been sacked and is deserted and the vessels of the Egyptians are carrying off all that was in it."

This news, implying the death of his queen, naturally caused deep mourning on the part of the king. Then the most eminent of the Persian nobles also proceeded to mourn, "in semblance for Statira, but each for his own woe," one for his wife, another for his sister, another for his daughter, each and every one for some one of his own. But though their enemies had sailed away, it was unknown to them in what direction over the sea they had gone.

On the second day, the ships of the Egyptians were seen approaching. The true state of affairs was of course unknown and they were astonished at the sight. Their confusion was intensified, moreover, by the raising from Demetrius' ship of the colors, which customarily are flown only when the king is on board; and this move, implying the presence of the enemy, aroused consternation. So running with all speed to Artaxerxes, they reported, "The chances are that some new king of Egypt is going to be discovered!"

He started up from his throne and hurried to the seashore and proceeded to give the signal for battle. To be sure, he did not have any war vessels, but he stationed all his forces at the shore prepared to fight. They were already bending their bows and were on the point of launching their spears, when Demetrius took in the situation and reported it to the queen. Statira then came out from under her canopy and showed herself, and at once they threw down their arms and bowed reverently before her.

The king could not restrain himself, but before the vessel had been warped to the shore, he was the first to leap upon it. Casting his arms about his queen, he wept with joy.

"What heavenly power has restored you to me, my darling wife!" he said. "It is simply beyond belief either that my queen should have been lost, or that once lost, she should have been found again. How is it that when I left you on the land, I should get you back from the sea?"

"You have me as a gift from Callirhoe," replied Statira.

On hearing that name, the king suffered, as it were, a fresh blow upon an old wound, and, with a glance at the eunuch, Artaxates, he said, "Take me to Callirhoe and let me thank her."

But Statira said, "You shall learn everything from me," and at the same time they proceeded from the harbor to the palace. Then, after ordering all the rest to go away and only the eunuch to remain with them, she narrated the happenings in Aradus and in Cyprus, and finally gave him Chaereas' letter.

On reading it, the king was filled with an infinite variety of emotions. The fact was, that while he was angered because of the capture of his dear ones, he was sorry that he had forced Chaereas to desert him; and on the other hand again he was grateful to him for removing the possibility of seeing Callirhoe any more. But above all else, he was seized with envy, and muttered, "Happy Chaereas, he is luckier than I!"

When they had their fill of recounting their experiences, Statira said, "Your Majesty, comfort Dionysius, for such is Callirhoe's request."

Accordingly Artaxerxes turned to the eunuch and said, "Have Dionysius come here."

So he came at once in high hopes, knowing nothing of what Chaereas had done, and thinking that Callirhoe, too, was with the rest of the women, and that the king was calling him to give him the girl as a reward for his valor. But when he came in, the king narrated to him all that happened from the beginning. At this crisis Dionysius manifested most clearly indeed both his good sense and his extraordinary self-discipline. Just as if a man should refuse to be disturbed when a thunderbolt fell at his feet, so he, on hearing words more startling than any thunderbolt—namely, that Chaereas was taking back Callirhoe to Syracuse—nevertheless kept his poise and, since the queen had been rescued, considered any expression of grief unsafe.

"If it were in my power," said Artaxerxes, "I should have restored Callirhoe to you, Dionysius, for you have fully demonstrated your good will and loyalty toward me. But since this is impossible, I bestow upon you the supreme command over all Ionia, and the honor of being enrolled as 'chief benefactor' to the royal house."

Dionysius bowed low and, after expressing his thanks, hastened to leave, so as to be free to vent his grief in tears. As he went out, Statira quietly handed him the letter.

When he had gone home and had shut himself up alone, recognizing Callirhoe's writing, he first kissed the letter, then opening it, he folded it to his heart as though she herself were there, and so held it for a long time, unable to read because of his tears. As soon as he had finished weeping, he began with difficulty to read it, and the first thing he did was to kiss Callirhoe's name. But when he came to "Dionysius, my benefactor," he sighed regretfully.

"It isn't 'my husband' any more," he said. "Really you are the one who is 'my benefactor.' What have I ever done for you, to earn that name?"

Nevertheless he was pleased with the apology the letter contained and read these words again and again, for they suggested that she had left him unwillingly. Love is just as buoyant as that, and can readily convince a man that his affection is returned.

Catching sight of his little son, he rocked him in his arms and said, "Some time, my baby, you too shall go home to your mother; she has told you so herself. But I shall live all alone, with no one to blame for all this but myself. My stupid jealousy has ruined me, and so have you, too, Babylon!"

With these words he made his preparations to travel back as quickly as possible to Ionia, finding comfort in the length of the journey, in his authority as ruler over many cities, and in the statues of Callirhoe in Miletus.

Such, then, was the condition of affairs in Asia. Meantime, in spite of his constant fear that once more some cruel divinity might attack him, Chaereas had completed his voyage to Sicily successfully, inasmuch as the wind stood continually at the stern and he was making the crossing in large vessels. But when Syracuse hove in sight, he gave orders to the captains to decorate the vessels, and, the sea being calm, to sail in together in massed array.

When people saw them from the city, they said, "Whose warships are these sailing in? Surely they are not from Athens. Come, let us bring the news to Hermocrates."

The report was made at once.

"General," they said, "consider well what you intend to do. Are we to close the harbors or open them up? We do not know, of course, whether a larger force is following after, and these boats we see are only the advance guard."

Accordingly Hermocrates hurried down from the market place to the seashore and dispatched a rowboat to meet them. The messenger, drawing near, inquired who they were; but Chaereas ordered one of the Egyptians to answer, "We are traders sailing in from Egypt, carrying a cargo which will delight the Syracusans."

"Well, don't sail in all at once," he said, "until we find out if you are speaking the truth. Those are no cargo boats which I see, but tall ships and apparently war vessels, so let most of them stay out at sea beyond the harbor, and bring in only one."

"Very well," they replied.

So Chaereas' ship sailed in first. On the upper deck it had a canopy closed about with Babylonian tapestries. When it had cast anchor, all the harbor was filled with men, for the common crowd is naturally a creature of curiosity, and on this occasion they had more reasons than usual for gathering. On seeing the canopy, they thought it covered, not human beings, but some valuable cargo, and they predicted now one thing, now another, guessing everything except the truth. As a matter of fact, convinced as they were by now that Chaereas was dead, it was really incredible that he should be thought of as sailing home alive in the midst of such magnificence as that. Chaereas' parents, accordingly, would not even come out of the house, but Hermocrates was still active in office, although he was in mourning, and he had taken his place on this occasion, albeit unobtrusively.

Amid the general mystification and straining of eyes, suddenly the tapestries were drawn aside, and Callirhoe was seen, clothed in Tyrian purple, and reclining on a gold-wrought couch, and Chaereas was sitting beside her in the uniform of a general. Never did a stroke of lightning or a crash of thunder so startle the eyes and ears of the spectators! Never did anyone who had discovered a treasure shout so loudly as the crowd did then at this unexpected sight! Words fail to describe it.

Hermocrates leaped aboard and ran to the canopy, and embracing his daughter, he cried, "My child, are you really alive or am I deceived in this, too?"

"Yes, father, I am—really so now that I have seen you alive."

In the midst of their joy, tears came to the eyes of all.

Meantime Polycharmus sailed in with the other ships. He personally had been intrusted with the rest of the fleet when it left Cyprus, because Chaereas could no longer spare time for any other purpose than to be alone with Callirhoe. Quickly, then, the harbor was filled and took on the appearance which it had after the victory over the Athenians; indeed, these vessels, too, were sailing home from battle, wreathed in victory and under the command of a Syracusan leader. The voices of those on the sea who called greetings to friends on shore were mingled with the seaward-returning shouts of the latter. Blessings, cheers, and prayers came thick and fast from each in turn.

Meantime Chaereas' father arrived, carried on a litter and fainting from unexpected joy. Chaereas' young comrades and fellow athletes were milling about in their eagerness to greet him, while the women surrounded Callirhoe. Even to their eyes, too, it seemed that Callirhoe had grown more lovely, so that in all honesty you would have said that it was Aphrodite herself whom you saw arising from the sea.

Chaereas came up to Hermocrates and to his father and said, "Here is the wealth of the Great King; take it."

At once he gave orders to unload an unestimated quantity of silver and gold; next he showed the Syracusans ivory and amber and fine clothing and every sort of richness of material and of art, including the couch and the table of the Great King, so that the whole city was filled, not as previously after the Sicilian war with the poverty of Attica, but, strange as it may seem, with the spoils of Persia in time of peace.

Eager as they were to gaze at them and hear them speak, the crowd shouted with one accord, "Let us go out to the general assembly!" And in less time than it takes to tell, the theater was filled with men and women. But when Chaereas entered by himself, both men and women all protested loudly, "Call in Callirhoe!" So Hermocrates granted the people this favor, too, and brought in his daughter.

First of all the people lifted their eyes to heaven, and praised the gods, feeling an even greater sense of gratitude for this day than for that of their victory. Then alternately they divided, with the men cheering Chaereas and the women Callirhoe, and then in turn united again to cheer them both together, and found greater pleasure in that.

Since Callirhoe was worn out by her voyage and sufferings, they led her away from the theater as soon as she had expressed her happiness at returning home. But the crowd detained Chaereas, wanting to hear all he had to tell of his foreign wanderings. He began with the concluding episodes, unwilling to sadden his audience with the melancholy events which came first.

But the people kept urging him, "Start over again, we entreat you! Tell us everything; don't leave anything out."

Chaereas hesitated, naturally somewhat embarrassed at several matters which had not turned out as he had intended, but Hermocrates said, "My son, do not be ashamed, even if you have something quite painful and disagreeable to tell us. Now that the end has proved glorious, it overshadows all that has gone before, but if you say nothing, that means that we will suspect something even worse from your silence. You are talking to your native city and to your parents, whose affection toward both of you is equally matched.

"Now even the people know the first part of your story already. They themselves brought about your wedding, you know. As for the plot of the rival suitors to arouse your unfounded jealousy, and how you rashly struck your wife, we all know that; and also the fact that after her seeming death she was given a splendid funeral, and that you, when brought to trial for murder, voted against yourself and wanted to die with your wife. Nevertheless, the people acquitted you, realizing that what had happened was not intended.

"Also they have reported to us the events that followed; how the grave-robber, Theron, dug his way into the tomb by night, and found Callirhoe alive, and putting her with the funeral offerings on his pirate ship, sold her into Ionia; how you set out in search of your wife and failed to find her, but falling in with the pirate ship at sea, you found the other pirates dead of thirst; how you brought Theron, the only one still alive, before our assembly and he, confessing under torture, was impaled upon the cross; how the city dispatched a warship with ambassadors to search for Callirhoe, and your friend, Polycharmus, sailed with you of his own accord—these things we know. But you must tell us what happened after your voyage from here."

Chaereas, taking his cue from this, proceeded with his story.

"We sailed safely across the Ionic Gulf and put in at the estate of a man of Miletus, named Dionysius, who is the superior of all the Ionians in wealth, lineage and fame. He it was who had bought Callirhoe from Theron for a thousand pieces of silver. Do not be startled! She did not become a slave; in fact, soon after he bought her he appointed her the mistress of his house and, though in love with her, was not rash enough to force his will upon a well-born girl; on the other hand, he could not endure to send the woman he loved back to Syracuse. When Callirhoe discovered that she was with child by me, wishing to preserve a future citizen for you, she felt compelled to marry Dionysius, and disguised the parentage of the child so that he might seem to be the son of Dionysius and so be brought up in a worthy manner. Yes, my friends of Syracuse! A fellow-citizen of yours there in Miletus is being brought up to a position of wealth by an illustrious gentleman. And indeed Dionysius' family is illustrious, and Greek as well; let us not begrudge him his great inheritance.

"This, to be sure, I learned later. At that time when I landed at this rural estate, I was in high hopes, simply because I saw a statue of Callirhoe in a temple. But during the night some Phrygian robbers rushed down to the seashore and fired our ship; they slaughtered most of us, and sold Polycharmus and me in chains to Caria."

At this a groan burst forth from the crowd, and Chaereas said, "Allow me to pass over what came next; it is sadder than what has gone before."

But the crowd shouted, "Tell us everything!"

So he continued, "The man who bought us, a servant of Mithridates, the governor-general of Caria, gave orders to set us digging with our feet in chains. When certain of the prisoners had murdered the guard, Mithridates ordered us all to be crucified. I was already being taken off when Polycharmus, threatened with torture, mentioned my name and Mithridates recognized it. You see, he had been a guest of Dionysius in Miletus and was present at the funeral of Chaereas; for Callirhoe, on learning of the business of the warship and the pirates, and thinking that I was dead, had erected an elaborate tomb for me. And so Mithridates at once gave orders to have me taken down from the cross—and I had almost come to my finish by then—and held me in great affection.

"He tried hard to restore Callirhoe to me and had me write a letter to her. Through the carelessness of the person in charge of it, Dionysius himself got the letter. He couldn't believe that I was alive, but instead he believed that Mithridates was plotting against his wife and at once he dispatched to the king a letter accusing Mithridates of adultery. The king admitted the case to trial and summoned us all to him. So we went inland to Babylon. Well, Dionysius brought Callirhoe with him and so made her the admiration and wonder of all Asia, while Mithridates took me along. When we got there, we pleaded this important case before the king. To be sure, he acquitted Mithridates at once, but he promised a further settlement between Dionysius and me regarding my wife, and meantime placed Callirhoe in the care of the queen, Statira.

"Gentlemen of Syracuse, how many times do you suppose I determined to die, parted as I was from my wife—and would have, if Polycharmus, my only loyal friend among them all, had not come to my rescue! The fact was, that the king completely neglected the case, being ardently in love with Callirhoe. However, he attempted neither seduction nor violence.

"Just in time, Egypt revolted and started a serious war which resulted in great good fortune to me. The queen took Callirhoe along with her, but I heard a false report from someone who said that she had been given over to Dionysius, and so, wanting to revenge myself upon the king, I deserted to the Egyptian king and performed some great deeds. I actually subdued Tyre myself, impregnable as it was, and then being appointed admiral, I defeated the Great King on the sea and became master of Aradus, where the king had left behind both his queen and all this wealth which you have seen. Thus I could even have made the Egyptian king master of all Asia, if he had not been killed, fighting apart from myself.

"As for the rest, I made the Great King your friend by restoring his queen as a gift to him, and by sending back their mothers, sisters, wives, and daughters to the highest Persian nobles. I myself have brought back here my noble Greeks and those of the Egyptians who wished it. Sometime another expedition of yours shall sail from Ionia and its leader shall be the grandson of Hermocrates!"

Prayers for the fulfilment of this ensued from the lips of all.

But Chaereas checked their shouts and said, "Both Callirhoe and I offer our thanks in your presence to Polycharmus, our friend. He has indeed shown the truest kindness and loyalty toward us, and if you consent, let us give him my sister as his bride, and for a dowry he shall have a share of the spoils."

The people confirmed this with a shout, "Noble Polycharmus! Faithful friend! The people are grateful to you. You have served your native land in a manner worthy of Hermocrates and Chaereas."

After this Chaereas spoke again: "And as for these three hundred Greeks, my valiant band, I beg you, make them your fellow citizens."

Again the people shouted assent, "You are worthy to share our citizenship; let this be put to the vote."

A decree was enacted and the three hundred at once took their seats as a part of the assembly. Chaereas also made each a present of a thousand pieces of silver, and to the Egyptians Hermocrates assigned a portion of land so that they could be farmers.

While the crowd was in the theater, Callirhoe, before entering her house, came up to Aphrodite's temple. Grasping the feet of the goddess and placing her face upon them, with her hair loosened, she kissed them and said, "My thanks to thee, Aphrodite! Once again thou hast shown me Chaereas here in Syracuse where as a girl I saw him at thy wish. I offer thee no reproaches, mistress, for what I have suffered; such was my fate. I beg thee, never again part me from Chaereas, but grant us both a happy life, and death together."

Such is my story about Callirhoe.